THE ACT OF SOLVING INTERPERSONAL PROBLEMS

8 STEPS TO CREATING A FORMIDABLE TEAM

IN A FEW HOURS

ROBERT B. KARGBO, PH.D.

THE ACT OF SOLVING INTERPERSONAL PROBLEMS
8 Steps to Creating a Formidable Team in a Few Hours

Copyright © 2021 Robert B. Kargbo, Ph.D.

All rights reserved. No portion of this book may be reproduced or stored in a retrieval system or translated in any form or by any means – electronic, mechanic, photocopy, recording, scanning, or other – except for brief quotations in critical reviews or articles, without the prior written permission of the author.

DEDICATION

This book is dedicated to my wife, Kumba Kargbo, children and extended family members.

TABLE OF CONTENTS

DEDICATION iii

Chapter 1	How Do You Uncover The Needs Of Your Team?	1
Chapter 2	The Act Of Becoming An Informed Leader	7
Chapter 3	Unlocking The Secrets Of Cohesive Team Building	15
Chapter 4	Have You Uncovered Why You Exist In The First Place?	23
Chapter 5	How Has The Outside World Defined You?	35
Chapter 6	Have You Been Able To Utilise The Clues On Your Path?	49
Chapter 7	Who Inspires You To Take Action?	61
Chapter 8	What Are The Thought Processes Holding You Back?	71
Chapter 9	Do You Know That Every Need You Have Can Be Transformed?	83
Chapter 10	What Are You Not Proud Of?	93
Chapter 11	Finding The Opportunity In Every Situation	104
Chapter 12	Transformational Leadership Doesn't Have To Be A Nightmare	119
Chapter 13	You've Just Unlocked The Secrets Of Great Leadership	123

Acknowledgment 126

About The Author 127

CHAPTER 1

HOW DO YOU UNCOVER THE NEEDS OF YOUR TEAM?

Did you know that 58% of people say they trust strangers more than their bosses? This shocking statistic existed before the pandemic, and how they managed to fare during the crisis became a source for concern. How can supervisors address employees' need when 89% of their bosses wrongfully believe their employers quit because they wanted more money? The truth is only 12% of employees leave an organization for more money. The dissatisfaction in the workplace is not only limited to one country. Global research has discovered that 79% of people who quit their jobs cite 'lack of appreciation' as their reason for leaving. The disconnect between employees and their supervisors is exacerbated by the fact that we are all unique and have different needs that should be addressed daily.

How often do we take the time to understand each other's needs in the workplace? We are constantly driven towards more productivity and more creativity. It is always more and more, without pausing to ascertain what makes one happy, or blossom in their work and personal life. We are constantly exposed to training that doesn't get to the core of our individual needs and doesn't address when we are not getting along with our supervisor. The solutions are general and superficial. They are geared towards checking the box and protecting the institutions rather than protecting our individual lives and integrity. Come to think of it, it is the individual employees/supervisors that make the institutions. Without the employees/supervisors, there will be no institution. If there is one, then it will not be fulfilling the needs of its customers. What this has led to sadly is unnecessary stress and frustration. Where employees/supervisors should be thriving, they are instead made to face destructive competition, envy, and unappreciation of the countless hours devoted to the workplace.

To feel appreciated goes beyond just using words, which most often replaces real tangible micro-actions that may be needed when there is a crisis. When things are going fine, it is easy to feel good and most of the problems or strife can be easily hidden. However, all the hidden grudges and hatred are manifested when problems arise. What happens to all the good things that have been said in the past? What happens to all the promises that were made in the past? Why should memories of all the good times just disappear with a flip of the switch? There is little remembrance of all the energy that has been put in all the years or months to make things good. We are remembered for who we are today and not what we were yesterday. Should it be that way? Does our value diminish once we pass a given day? That cannot be true in any way. How can we keep that value in the good times or the bad times? We cannot be valuable today and be valueless the next day. There must be ways to fix this and this is what we talk about in this book. We have constantly applied theoretical approaches to most problems and yet we are continuously divided. Why do all the advanced degrees and classes not prepare us for the level of stress we face in real life or the workplace? We often deal with the symptoms of the problems rather than look at their root causes. Granted, the real root cause is individually based. It makes a lot of sense why the solution cannot be found in the general classes that are geared towards helping the average person. **Well, you are not an average person. You are a unique individual**

that needs a unique solution. So, why go through all the motions of an average person when there is so much value you can offer? The system, with no fault of its own, cannot afford to deal with you as an individual. It will be impossible to fulfill all our individual needs and the system will collapse if that were the case.

I have witnessed countless situations where employees and supervisors are in a harmonious relationship that fosters productivity, perfect work-life balance, happiness, and so forth. How will you feel to be in such a situation compared to the constant strife or argument about who is right? A situation where all preferences are put aside and we can see the value we bring to each other rather than the things we want to fix in each other. Many things need to be fixed, but should that be the constant focus? What about the things that we already have that could easily fix what we don't have? The fact is a general consideration will not get us to our preferred situation unless our interests are addressed. There is incredible power that keeps man and the world in place. We don't often consider this power, but we constantly pay attention to the very weak force that divides us. Yes, I indicate 'weak force that divides' as we are generally thought to be the most powerful force, which cannot be further from the truth. Just because the sun is absent at some point doesn't mean it is weak but that we have not utilized it fully in a way that converts the enormous energy to useful purpose. The power that keeps us together is just unlimited and the more we learn to earnest it the more we enjoy its value. In general, we don't leave our homes or workplaces to wilfully be nuisances or troublemakers in any way. Why do we often perceive another person to be such and refuse to consider that it was never the intention in the first place? If we could consider that at all times, there will be so much empathy, enhanced productivity and minimization of needless stress and frustration.

In the next chapter, I will share proven results of how supervisors/employees have been transformed by applying the simple but effective principles that you will read about in this book. There are, of course, many solutions to many problems and there is not a one-size-fits-all paradigm. However, some things are ascribed to all of us, no matter our status or circumstances. When we can figure that out, it is unimaginable what we can do together. It is also unimaginable how a situation that is considered hopeless can be transformed into hopefulness and continue to thrive.

CHAPTER 2

THE ACT OF BECOMING AN INFORMED LEADER

The end-of-year evaluation was a tense time, as we all looked forward to being rewarded or being punished for not doing well in the previous year. As a supervisor, I wasn't immune to the anxiety. What has my direct reports said about me? Is there any situation that has not turned-out well that I am unaware of? What about my supervisor? Where their customer expectations that I did/didn't fulfill? I had two groups to supervise in a tense and high scientific productivity environment. In this setting, making many mistakes is not an option. You cannot afford to lag while others are progressing. Have my direct reports been truthful about the performance they said they were impressed by? After the usual praise for my efficiency, productivity, and having the most productive group in the department, we encountered a problem, and it was not a common problem. I was told that 'every member of my team is not only productive but they seem to be very happy. What can I do to turn it down a little?' I was mesmerized by such a statement. I responded that we do everything in our power to make sure we are happy and productive while we work. How can I turn it down when people are feeling fulfilled by what they do?

Not All Your Visionary Plans Will Be Understood By Others

We are trying hard to find meaning and purpose in what we do in life. So, how can I tune down when we have found a purpose in our work? The concept you will read about in this book is so effective that people find it unbelievable and sometimes are not prepared to witness the results. They may assume it is a fluke and unsustainable. But I was very certain about the results they were seeing.

I took every one of those direct reports as individuals. I had the highest respect for each of them. I told them that science is generally difficult. If it were easy, then, all of us will be out of our respective jobs because we would have solved all the problems that existed in the world.

Sometimes, people want everything to be easy, but what they should be interested in is finding meaning and value in what they are doing. Why are they doing what they are doing? What is their purpose in the job they have and how is that value seen each day? The problem the company had to deal with was, people were trying to join my team and management was pressurized and didn't know what to do. Meanwhile, I wasn't aware of behind the scene lobby that was taking place. To me, I was doing nothing special because all I did was to apply the very simple and basic principles I had gathered along the way in my career and early life. How did I get to the point where my supervising role was so outstanding? Was I born that way?

The Simple Answer Is A Resounding NO.

I was a very troubled kid growing up. In fact, I was short-tempered. I hated waiting for results and was anxious to respond to every situation. I couldn't give praise easily because I felt deprived and unfulfilled in my life. There was so much need that I couldn't imagine how others were getting ahead while I was behind. Lifting others was not natural because my own needs were unfulfilled and beyond the average kids. They say when life gives you lemons, you can choose to give it up, let it be, or turn it into lemonade. Being there, was what I needed to transform and reinvent myself in my personal life and my career.

It was a transformational moment when I realized my lifestyle wasn't going to take me anywhere, and if I wanted to succeed, I had to make drastic changes. If the external world doesn't have a solution for me and the world seems to be like a wilderness, I have to turn internally and figure out how to interact with my fellow human beings no matter how difficult that might be. Is there something unique to each of us that I can figure out? How can I adjust my behavior to allow others to help me in life? How do I quickly figure out the wheat from the chaff? How can I imagine what others are thinking and be able to respond or behave accordingly? This is often branded as emotional intelligence. I will testify that nature has given us an abundance of emotional intelligence for everyone to grab from. As they say, the most useful things in life are free for all to take. It is human nature to take for granted what we can get easily, such as the air we breathe, the water we drink, the activities of daily living that we experience. The value quickly comes in when we are deprived of such abundance and when for example, we are sick and are unable to enjoy such amenities. That is when we realize they are extremely useful, even though they are free gifts.

No Doubt, Every One Of Us Has An Internal GPS

Once I realized that interacting with others was the only way to get me from point A to point B, I started self-reflecting each day. Each evening, I would reflect on all my interactions for the day. I took note of my harsh responses, things I said that were disrespectful, instances where I was ungrateful, where I was rushing to talk, and so forth. I took note of the behaviors I needed to improve upon and reminded myself over and over during the day to adjust accordingly. For me, it was an organic exercise and nothing I read was motivating enough than my desire to succeed and that there was no apparent second option. Self-reflection is one of humanity's greatest gifts, freely available to all but something that we are scared to face. Most often when we face self-reflection, we may easily excuse ourselves and rationalize our behaviors and responses. If everything that we do is perfect, how can we make meaningful adjustments? It is something that gets absorbed in our busy schedule as we stay focused on trying to figure out the next best thing. We are constantly in a hurry to outdo the biggest star or competition.

One big advantage to the practice of self-reflection was training my brain to recall things. It is scientifically proven that the more we train our brain to recall events, the more effective it becomes in storing and recalling what we are exposed to or what we learn. Looking back, I realize that I am still benefiting from that early foundation. Not only was I taking note of what I was doing but what others were doing as well. With time, it became clear that no matter who the individual is, we are all connected in a very powerful way if we can simply align who we are to who others are. It looks like a cliché but it has to be emphasized that just knowing this and not putting it into practice is a waste of time.

How can you use these tools that can very well transform not only your own life but the lives of those around you, including your direct report(s) or co-workers? You have what it takes to do what you will read in this book because it is within every person's reach.

If I could help transform workers that others have given up on into people moving on the right path and have completely turned around, I believe you can do much more. The path to success needs a willing heart and the motivation to see the best in you and others around you.

In addition to the foundation of my childhood, I have obtained professional human development on the job. This training has solidified my character and made it easy to communicate and simplify the things that you will gain in this book. There are scientific lessons that have corroborated these principles that you will read. I was hesitant to talk about these principles until I was sufficiently exposed to the scientific principles of human psychology and behavior. It was illuminating to realize these scientific principles are there for all of us to adopt but we often fail to make the connection between the daily interactions we have and the outcome of those human interactions. How do we harness these principles to our advantage and make them work for us? Let's briefly touch on each of those principles.

CHAPTER 3

UNLOCKING THE SECRETS OF COHESIVE TEAM BUILDING

To succeed in our careers and life, in general, requires so much hard work, tenacity, consistency but the question is, does it have to be painful? Does it have to be unreachable by anyone that is determined to succeed? Who would be happy to have a project they've put so much effort into only for it to be derailed? Who does not want to succeed in whatever they do, especially after they've put so much effort into it? The scientific and interactional complexity of human beings is a pointer to how badly mother nature wishes for our success. It will make no sense for that not to be the case. The main barrier is that we never take the time to truly understand how special we are. We will look at that in detail in Chapter 4.

Sometimes We Need To Step Back

Once we begin to step back, we start to understand why we are here in the first place. The more proofs we see confirming our existence, the more we will be able to connect with every moment and then, every interaction becomes more meaningful. We can easily see the 'why' that influences our jobs. The 'why' to our career. The 'why' to so many situations. The irony is that there is so much scientific evidence that backs who we are and how we can harness the value we bring in our work places and social lives. In Chapter 5, we will take a deeper dive into how we can connect with who we are from the outside.

What Lessons Have You Learned In Every Interaction You've Had?

Many incidences have taken place in the past, incidences that we don't fully understand why they happened in the first place. Other times, when we look back on certain situations, we gain a clearer understanding, and many times, what comes to mind is 'if I knew this was going to happen, I could have done X, Y, Z.' We often regret not knowing how to respond or the inability to connect the dots at the time. What about if you have the clarity you need to connect what happened in our past at our workplaces or our social lives? And also find a clue that could bring us hope and direction? Many situations in our past could bring hope for the future. How do you decipher that? We will look at that in Chapter 6.

We All Have Come Across So Many People In Our Life And Career

Most often, we interact with people briefly in our lives. Who among them is meant to provide a guide to our life? Who among them is meant to inspire your career or personality? Some may have been people that we read about in history books or people that may be around us. It could be our previous supervisor or teacher that has inspired us in the past. How do we connect in such a way that their story is an inspiration to our lives? How can we discard very quickly interactions that are not geared towards moving us forward in our careers or lives? How can we take each interaction and quickly turn the bad ones into ones that bring hope to our lives? We will examine that in Chapter 7.

We Are Human Beings With So Many Scientific Complexities

There are things that we are prone to. No matter how powerful we become or how rich we are, many involuntary actions take place that are not dependent on our will. For example, your heartbeat that circulates the blood in your veins keeps moving even if you are not paying attention to it. If it were dependent upon us paying attention to it every second, then sleeping would be impossible. There will be no way to stay alive because it is just impossible to maintain. There are innate actions or intentions that we are born with. The fight for survival is an innate attribute we cannot deny or ignore. Many times, the intent to be negative is instantaneous. We are just prone to looking for things that do not function well and criticize them negatively because there might be a better way. It turns out that to improve our lives, we become dependent on such interactions. The question is how can we do that without it being a burden to our lives? How can we do that without it being frustrating or depressing? We are caught in this web of negative intent and are unable to dissociate from it. Others may not entirely pick it up but you know deep down that it exists. So, how can we turn it to our advantage? We will examine that in Chapter 8.

There Are Some People That We Can See They Are Always Happy Or Cheerful

Some will feel offended by such a posture. In fact, we are thought to be gritty, serious minded, professional and people have written about it as a way of boosting their efficiency and careers. The problem arises when we become so gritty that it becomes embedded in our psyche and we are unable to turn the clock around. We become so gritty that every situation becomes that and we can no longer step back and enjoy every moment that we find ourselves in. Why should just being unhappy make something work more efficiently? It may work for some people but I don't believe it should be the case for everyone. We are all striving to find meaning in what we do. How do we then find that meaning and are not able to enjoy it? How can we use positive intent to our advantage and harness the guidance that we can find in our career or life? We will examine such positive intent in Chapter 9.

The Ability To Have Good Intention To Things Are Unavoidable

How do we respond to such intentions? As you may imagine, there can be negative or positive responses. Often, the ones that we are most concerned with are the negative responses. In certain cases, we have zero control over these negative responses. We may have been trapped in a pattern or cycle where it is an auto-response. How can we recognize these negative responses and find a way to deal with them? How can we turn such responses into a lesson that provides a path to our next interaction? Many classes have been taught on how to do that. I believe often, they are addressed from a superficial point of view and we get only the immediate benefit that fades away with time. There are ways to make those changes permanent or for the most part, predictable and so we are better prepared to turn them around when they occur. We will examine the negative responses in Chapter 10.

How We Respond Could Be More Important Than The Desired Outcome

There are times our responses will not make sense but if it is an accurate or positive response to the situation, the benefit or reward may come later. I know we have been conditioned to always look for immediate rewards. The fact is that life is so complex, how then can we intellectualize every response and understand every result? There is no way to respond to things positively and then fully actualize every immediate reward at the same time. Sometimes, responding positively may make no sense. How can I give someone a second chance when I have warned them about the situation and even written down what they should do?

The amount of time spent on preventing an individual from exhibiting a particular behavior can be enormous and if the individual has an addictive behavior that you are not aware of, there is no way to decipher that and our expectations for this individual may be very high. What if this individual just needs one last chance to have a complete turnaround? How can we know that and be empathetic? How can we know that the challenges at the place of work or in our career just need one more positive response? What about if you get so close to figuring out your purpose in life by just allowing that one more positive response?

A Positive Response Doesn't Mean We Don't Take Things Seriously

We don't have to be sad for others to take us seriously. Our ability to stay happy and respond positively when everything around us is saying the opposite is an admirable trait. In our world today, occasions for negative responses abound. There is so much trouble, offensive people, negative news stories, and stories about wicked and unsympathetic people in the world today. In fact, we are all prone to the hype. If the news is boring, then we turn it off. If a story is boring, we become uninterested in what is being said. We all look for a story that is exciting, fulfilling, and has a happy ending, the one that motivates us. It is difficult to dissociate what we are experiencing from what our next move has to be in our life. How can we peel the onion to see the things that we ought to be seeing? We will examine that in detail in Chapter 11.

CHAPTER 4

HAVE YOU UNCOVERED WHY YOU EXIST IN THE FIRST PLACE?

Imagine how successful we have all become in this modern era because of all the discoveries we didn't even know were possible a few years ago. Such accomplishments tend to drive us into thinking forward at full speed and using all the motivation we can find to do more and more. Amid such success, there are always hidden dangers and circumstances that are very painful to watch and they come with needless suffering, pain, anxiety, and so forth. The question is, should it be that way? What can we do to alter such a situation? Can it be a win-win situation? The answer to these questions, I will leave to the reader to discern for themselves. However, a spoiler alert; Yes, it can be avoided or prevented. Let me start by focusing on what we have generally abandoned and ignored. There is a saying that 'If we do not know where we are coming from, how can we know where we are going?' This is an important question that everyone should ask themselves. Where are we coming from? To bring it home, to you the reader, where are you coming from? Many people will answer this question differently by referring to their birthplaces, their cities, their home addresses, etc. These are the general answers we often provide that do not get at the essence of the question. To get at something substantial, we must go back and recall the circumstances that led to our existence.

A Snapshot Of History Shows A Single Cell That You And I Came From

Who or what decided the existence of that cell? Can we slow ourselves down and ask this fundamental but crucial question? Again, many people will point to their father or mother. This is just a standard answer that doesn't provide a substantial answer but the superficial one. If it was only my father and mother that was the deciding factor, why do we have millions of people who want children but do not have them? Can we show them the guaranteed formula for finding one? My point is, it takes more than that and we often forget that the process is so complex because even during cell division, mistakes could happen that could result in painful or admirable genetic mutations.

How many of us as an individual can we find operating in our city, state, country, world, or universe? The law of demand and supply states that the rarer a commodity, the more expensive it becomes. The question is, why don't we look at ourselves that way? We tend to leave the answers for others to define who we are, how special we are, or what we should become. It cannot be far from the truth. If these people or circumstances have the overall power to truly or permanently define who we are, why are we still struggling with the same things? I have watched with empathy how frustrating people can become once they allow people to define their capabilities for them.

Do Not Let Your Circumstances Define You

If our circumstances define us, we will be constantly stunted in our growth. There is no problem that you can ever face or have ever faced that will trump the circumstances the single-cell went through to bring you where you are. We can only make conscious efforts to think about it over and over until it becomes a part of ourself. It is imperative that if this will be beneficial to you, you must not over-analyze things. Albert Einstein is often credited as saying, 'It is insanity to do the same thing over and over again and expect a different result.' You may have put in so much energy at your workplace and have continuously been looking for recognition or appreciation. The question is, are you just doing the same thing over and over again? Is the mindset just the same or are you looking for a different way to come up with a different result? Every aspect of what I am talking about is proven to work all the time if applied correctly. I can attest to that from a first-hand experience and you will find examples in this book. We cannot allow ourself to be defined by others, it will always be a struggle or could lead to a tragedy. Why don't we take the first step to ruminate on what science has said about us?

For the non-scientific mind, look at the millions of people in a crowd. How come you are reading this book when millions of others are reading different things? What made you read this book? Was it by mistake? What are the odds that you could have picked up some other book? If you recall how you got this book, it would be similar to what a scientific mind would think. So, the principles are still the same and that is why what I am talking about applies to both scientific and non-scientific mind. It is easy for me to correlate what is happening to the scientific principles that I have come to appreciate. However, it doesn't make it more or less truthful.

These Are The Principles That Are Guaranteed To Work Irrespective Of The Person Or Circumstance

It is tantamount to trying to go up. The natural laws state that if you do nothing to stay up, you will definitely come down because of gravity. That is ingrained in our psyche but it gets completely lost when it comes to things that will make us successful. The conscious effort to take the time to understand how special you are will pay in an incredibly helpful way. The time you spent will pay off multiple times and you will gain a lot more leisure time.

The fact that you feel less energized doesn't mean that you don't have enough energy to fuel your life's journey. Think about the atomic bomb; it has so much energy that the world believes that only a few people should have access to its secrets. Well, at first, no one understood how to harness that energy, but when we did, we found it incredible how we didn't spend so much time figuring it out earlier. We are seated with such incredible energy, that it will take a conscious effort to harness such power. Even if you don't trust what you are capable of, you can trust what you are reading. You can implement it, so you can come out of any challenge. The energy some people have always found after their self-discovery has been transformational. Many people didn't have all the tools to deal with life's complexities but they have triumphantly overcome their work-challenges and are now finding life more fulfilling.

What Are The Benefits Of Knowing Our Limitations?

Even though we want to have all the benefits, we can also derive incredible benefits by accounting for our limitations. Reverting to who you are as a single cell should bring out some of the limitations that we need to recall and make a part of ourselves. Let it be part of our natural decision-making process. Telling anyone that, what works for me will 100% work for you is complete lunacy. Although we are made of the same chemical components, how we modulate those chemicals is crucial. We have the same starting materials to work with and it is guaranteed that when we handle some aspects of those materials correctly, we will produce the desired result. The opposite is also true. In recalling my limitations, I realized that once those cells began to divide and proliferate, I wasn't there to control them. Now, I can influence how those cells divide by controlling what I eat and what I do. The control is still limited by all measurements. We can only do the best we can to control those cells but it is not always successful.

My First Flight

My first flight happened when I was a teenager and it was very enjoyable. I enjoyed going through the thunderstorms. I even wished we went through it more often. I had limited information at the time because I wasn't exposed to the dangers that would unfold as a result of the turbulence. As I became more informed, I began to dread those moments. At one time, I became afraid to fly but I had to because of the nature of my job. I experienced a transformational moment when going through a storm in the air, and reminded myself about my teenage experience. After I had a monologue about how the dangers were really non-existent, I realized that I had only been influenced by the dreadful information I had absorbed in the past. I could do nothing to control the circumstance. The pilot and the crew are the only ones that could control the airplane. So, why don't I just relax and read a newspaper or book? Since that time, I have come to somehow enjoy flying. Saying it is the same as when I was a teenager will not be accurate. No matter how reckless we may think as adults, thinking about it as teenagers is very difficult. We have come to carry so many responsibilities - we don't want to be delayed or have our flight diverted, etc. Just carrying that weight creates challenges by themselves. It is not easy to switch and say, 'I don't care what happens to me on this flight.' Having said that, we can learn to simply enjoy the moment.

How Often Do You Reflect?

How often have we considered reflecting on our limitations or the circumstances that led to our existence or present circumstance? To encourage ourself, let's focus on that for a few weeks or as the circumstance permits and incorporate it into the principles we will find in the rest of this book. The fact is we don't need to set a dedicated time if we can't afford it at the moment. We can begin with the very small step, which is doing something about it no matter how small. You may want to write down what the journey you are embarking on is about. You are discovering who you really are. Some may have done this but it can't be the same all the time. It doesn't matter if you have done it in the past or not, the question is how useful has that circumstance or practice become? Has that helped your psyche in any way? It should propel you to do better daily. It is like that extra ingredient that seasons the recipe, without which it could still be good but not great.

Many people use powers beyond themselves to try to understand who they are. Why spend money on something that you can do for yourself? You are the master of your own universe but that doesn't mean you may have all the answers either. It doesn't mean you cannot or shouldn't learn from others. The important thing is if no individual ordered the cell to divide, how can they tell you who you are without first understanding you as an individual? Introspection will bring out your uniqueness. Some have come to rely on religious or non-religious direction. Irrespective of where you choose to begin, if you go in with a sincere mind, attitude and singularity of purpose, you will come out with great rewards. Why am I so emphatic? As a trained scientist, there are absolutes we don't use at all, if possible. I have used it here frequently knowing that they have been scientifically proven and naturally will deserve such emphasis.

You Are Validated The Way You Are

The same circumstance that requires a change in perspective should also help in looking at how we evaluate our successes. Success may not be something we see in our immediate future but sometimes, when we look back, we discover that our perspective has changed. The way we see ourselves is different. How can we measure it? For some, it will be easy since they can easily document where they were before their journey. For others, it may be challenging. That shouldn't change the result but it may reduce our appreciation of the transformation. If you are expecting an immediate transformation, you go by with the time and devotion you put into it. How you understand it will depend on how you purposefully think about it and practice the principles. If you are looking for others to validate your success, then you should remember they are also limited in their human ability. They cannot give what they don't have. Besides, as we overcome our limitations from time to time, we learn new things. Imagine submitting an assignment to a teacher. A teacher grades based on the information he/she may have. You can present the same question to another teacher with advanced information and get a lesser grade, just because he/she will look at it from a different perspective. How can you allow others to grade your own life?

We Are Indeed Trained To Be Highly Competitive

We are often worried about whether we are replaceable or whether others will outshine us at work. We have indeed been trained to eye-mark our competition, to always look out for ourselves. Though this counsel is meaningful, it will in time lose its fundamental value.

While we are so focused on what others are looking or doing, we forget the most powerful of competition, which is harnessing that incredible power and focus within. The moment that is lost, it will be the moment we become directionless. Then, it becomes power without purpose, strength without manifestation, beauty without admiration, purpose without character. No matter what can be replaced from the outside, there is no way it is replaceable from the inside. That is where no one has access to except you hand over the power to them.

If we know this fact and take it 'religiously' or if we are offered a million-dollar check to truly understand who we are, will we spend the effort and time to make it happen? The reality is that from the grand look of things, we'll be getting more than just crispy dollar bills. Imagine being free from the pain and suffering that comes when that focus is missing. Can we put a value on the loss in productivity? The sleepless nights? Anger or frustration when we constantly doubt our ability or who we are? The guiding principle is to bring back our focus to who we are and this can be enhanced by considering what we have been told or what we believe about ourselves.

CHAPTER 5

HOW HAS THE OUTSIDE WORLD DEFINED YOU?

Have you ever considered who you are? I know this question will bring about many answers. The typical response involves details like, 'I am very talented,' 'I have one/two or no kids,' 'My favorite colors are ---,' I owned many possessions etc. While these are all good answers, they never really answer the true question. What are the things that you have heard and have retained that influence your decision-making from time to time? The research that has been done on how our memory works indicates that there is a short-term memory and long-term memory of every second in our lives. In many instances, we recall certain old information that we had forgotten. Does it mean we lost it? No. It was retained somewhere until an external stimulus caused us to remember it. If we have experienced something like this before, will it be wrong to say that often, we recall information that we can trace back to an occasion we were once part of? Why is this aspect so critical? The straightforward answer is that it is incredibly important to recognize the negative or positive aspects in our lives that have shaped the way we accept or reject information. What we recall in challenging or critical situations will make all the difference how we respond. We may have been told that you need to stand up for yourself to succeed. The question is, when is a good time to stand up for one's self and when is a good time to back out? If we are going to get along with anyone in our lives, we must recognize this. Because we are more likely to interact with people that may have different perspectives and if we don't learn to back off sometimes, there will be no reconciliation in anything we do in life.

What Things Are Holding You Back?

What are the things that you may have been told in your childhood that you still recall? Some people may have found themselves in abusive environments as children due to no fault of their own. They were bullied and brought down. Some of these people believe that and allow that statement to influence them all through their adult lives. At certain times, they may recall those words and start to doubt their own abilities. If this person continues to experience it, it would have an incrementally devastating effect in the lifestyle they adopt.

How do we prevent these from having negative effects on our lives? Identifying a problem could be the first step towards solving it. What are those things that have been said to us in our childhood? Spending some time to think about it and try making a list will be most helpful and productive.

They may also include positive things too. How will positive things cause a problem if it is positive? The short answer is that the positive statements can also be as depressing as the negative statements. Imagine being told that you would be rich and famous. Although the dream of almost every parent is to see their child succeed, become famous, admired by all, and of immense value to humanity, but will we all be rich and famous? We know the answer but none of us will come to accept that as reality. Some people beat themselves up daily because they believe they haven't done anything worthwhile to become rich and famous. They obsess over stories of people who got rich or famous by accident or by simply an 'alignment with their stars.' There are many examples of people who have succeeded by putting aside such confidence in what they were told and putting in the effort to work very hard. The point is what we are told will continuously impact our behavior in one way or the other.

How Can You Stay Focus Amidst Challenges?

How do we carry that confidence and not give it up? It is important to recognize the problem but it is equally important to do something about it. Many are turned off when it comes to the 'doing' part. To some extent, they are right to feel that way because it is the difficult part. However, should that be the difficult part? I believe it should be the easy aspect if only we can align with who we are. And this we can do if we can take time to understand who we are from the inside as we've seen in Chapter 4. Before going to steps that we can take to figure out how we can turn the situation around, it is also important to discuss what we are being told from the outside as adults.

What are the things that you can recall during your adulthood that others have told you and that may have a positive or negative impact on your daily life? Your supervisor may have complimented you and you carry that compliment throughout your day. Unfortunately, not everyone has had a similar experience. Some may have had negative experiences with their supervisors or colleagues who didn't have many good things to say about them. As an adult, it can be confusing to decipher whether what is being said is genuine or not, because compliments are constantly being thrown around. How is that affecting our decision-making? The important aspect is to identify those things that may not align with the energy in our daily lives. Are their words draining our motivation? Is our present situation making work depressing? Is it making us hesitant to truly participate in what others are doing? Are we just going through the motions of belonging or trying to fit into the situation?

How can we change or transform that situation? How do we bring it to the attention of those that may be responsible for those feelings? It is easy to be angry and deal with the situation that may just make it worse rather than making it better. Some might argue that is the only way to produce the best results. From my experience, it is the most ineffective solution. What most often people get is a supposedly quick result that covers the problem, only for it to explode at the wrong place and the wrong time. The most effective way may seem slow in the beginning but once it is solidified, it will be very powerful and will knock out any stumbling block that will come our way.

What Is The Most Effective Way To Address The Problem?

Let us go back to our earlier question; what is the most effective way to address the problem? Also, bear in mind that you may be given the wrong compliment and you believe it is true, refusing to see the need to improve in that certain aspect. Constructive feedback could be very difficult to give. Others may quickly disagree. The missing link that is often ignored is that constructive feedback needs a solid foundation for it to be effective. If you wait only at the end of the year to receive constructive feedback, it may quickly become negative because it is easy to hang on to the one thing that needs improvement and quickly dismiss the hundreds of good that has been done. Having a solid foundation before constructive feedback is something we build daily or anytime we are at work. There are moments when things will go well and there will be many moments of uncertainty. In those moments, do we try to do the best we can in holding the good working relationships? These are the moments that completely weaken the foundation for constructive feedback.

We Cannot Eat Our Cake and Have It Back

We cannot be told we are good for nothing at the moment of crisis and then after the crisis, be told that you are the best worker. Will you ever believe that? How effective will it be when the same people attempt to give you constructive feedback? The little things will always make a significant difference. Who we are from the outside feeds on what we hear on a daily basis? List out the things you have heard from your colleagues and supervisor. Have a column for the positives and another for the negatives. The next thing will be to identify the ones that influence how we approach our daily duties. We may put them into categories. Once we identified them, the next step will be to ask ourselves what we can do about it? What we will do about them will only be effective if we purposefully take the right steps. It doesn't have to be major steps but it has to be purposeful. It will not just fix itself. Many people wrongly believe that after identifying the problem, they do not need to do anything about it. In some instances, they may be unsure of what they can do and believe that it is someone else's job to make the problem go away. In most cases, it is our approach to the problem that makes the difference.

How Can Asking The Right Question Get You To The Bottom Of The Problem?

What if the problem becomes very minimal and who we are from the outside becomes amplified, will that make any difference? What if that problem is the obstacle to our career? The question is, does that have to be the obstacle to our career? Are we paying attention to who we are? Why is that problem the decider of who we are from the inside? Where was that problem when we were born? Where was that problem when we were rescued from a bad situation? Where was that problem when we got our present jobs?

Could that problem be telling us that we have arrived at a point that will get us to the next level of success? Could that be a sign that we are ready for the next big thing? I believe that 99% of our problems occur when we are trying to move to our next level. The missing link is how we define our success. Does success mean more money? Does it mean fame? To be respected by our colleagues? It will be important to identify what success looks like to you. Success should come from within and not from the outside; that will only give you temporary compliments. In many instances, the compliment is so temporary that it doesn't get past a few days and we are back to the negative feelings. What about compliments that energize and propel us constantly? These are the compliments that will perfectly align with who we are from the inside.

After identifying all the possible categories, take the most important one. For example, if what others tell us continues to devastate us, how do we change that? If we recognize how much pain and suffering that has caused, then it will be easy to take it head-on. Science has told us that the most effective solutions are those that come from within. They are deliberate and they align with who we are. Think about the things that will counter the negative things you have carried along and influence how you feel. In the beginning, it may look like it is not working but that is not true. If we think about how long this has been going on, how do we imagine that it can just disappear? However, once we begin to give it that counterpunch, it nullifies the negative aspect. We will divert more energy to the positive aspect than the negative aspect. Most often how we get to process the problem makes all the difference. If we have come to conclude that the person causing the pain is not worthy of living, should they disappear from the workplace for the situation to change? Setting that expectation creates more pain when you see the person daily. However, we want to recognize that this individual could be trapped in their own problems and may not even be aware of a solution on their own. It may have little or nothing to do with us per se. We just happen to be in that situation at that particular time or work place.

You Didn't Decide To Be In It, In The First Place

I have seen many transformations where the receiver of negative feedback refused to believe it and stayed positive instead. Indeed, the most important response is to stay positive and align with who you are. It is also important to recognize that these individuals may require some empathy. Saying a person who has caused so much pain and suffering needs empathy may offend some people. Most people believe that such an individual deserves the worst. But empathy does not depend on what the individual deserves or doesn't deserve but most often it should be unaffected by how the person treats you. The ignorance on their part, thinking they will ultimately define who you are eventually is so wrong. Recall the things that were said about us and realize that most of it turned out to be completely false. Can we see the same things happening in this situation in the next few years? At this moment, the negative connotation may appear very powerful or destructive. It is important to also remember that they do not have the last say in what happens in our lives. We are much more deserving of a happy life, a fruitful career, and a satisfying workplace that provides support and comfort.

How Can We Counter Negative Thoughts?

What are the things that could help you counter the negative things that you have been told? Sometimes, we do all the right things in our workplaces but ignore them completely when it affects our lives outside the work place. This is one of the greatest mistakes most people often make. They may have taken into account what they need to do to deal with the challenges in their relationship but will ignore what they are hearing, reading, seeing or even participating in. Science has indicated with certainty that even though you claim to turn your brain off when you are outside the workplace, it is never off. The key is to recognize that applying the principles you have discovered will help your situation. With little or no educational resources as a child, I practiced physics by using woods or strings to understand the pulley system. We do that all the time but fail to apply the same principle when it comes to our workplaces.

We don't need to do anything extraordinary. All we may need to do is simply apply the principles to what we are doing at home, in our relationships and look for examples that reinforce what we are trying to achieve. It will change our situations, our perspectives, and bring the relief we are seeking, and it will begin to make that change that we thought was impossible. Believing that the problem will disappear simply by ignoring or confronting the situation violently will not solve or get to the root of the problem. Because if we believe and stay consistent in the situation, it will pay much more when there is harmony. Think about being empathetic to individuals that may be going through incredible suffering in their own lives and imagine that we are witnessing it first-hand. They will, of course, not acknowledge it. If they do, it will make it so much easier for us to see where they are coming from.

What About Seeing The Problems Before They Tell Us About Them?

This does not mean the problem will disappear the moment you talk to this person. The more you look at it that way the better you will be able to handle the situation. Think about the adult doing this right now. What if this person truly possesses a childlike mind? Will that not just begin to change our perspectives? If we consider that the person may be suffering from some form of mental illness, will that change our perspectives? If someone is clinically diagnosed to have a mental issue, it makes it easier to see where they are coming from. How many people do we interact with every day that should be in the system receiving treatment? We may even blame ourselves for not recognizing it early enough and taking responsibility. We know the system cannot be perfect but what if we find ways to minimize what others have come to instill in our psyche? We must refuse to be held back by the negative things we have come to internalize.

There have been great leaders in the past; what have they said that is still running our day-to-day lives? Have we considered influential people of faith? Some people respectfully don't want anything to do with faith. However, some people will consider themselves incomplete without invoking faith to overcome the negative parts of their life. Rather than trying to convince anyone about faith, I strongly believe that this perspective is helpful to everyone irrespective of their faith. Why could that be true? The word 'human being,' does it apply to any faith, religion, or belief? Does the brain care about all of the different aspects of our behavior or uses unique chemicals for all of our behavior? If the brain uses unique chemicals for each behavior, then our brains will be so big that we will be like the pigeons rubbing each other all the time. Nature has found efficiency by utilizing the same set of chemicals for all our interactions. So, what I am talking about applies to everyone. I may just need to use words that could relate better to the religious and the non-religious. If you don't want anything to do with belief, faith, or religion, you may skip the rest of this chapter. Although sometimes, seeing things from other perspectives may be very helpful. Imagine that the individual causing you pain at work is religious.

Our Connectedness

How can you expect to relate to that individual if you never try to see where they are coming from? He or she may be trapped in religion and doesn't even know how to navigate the secular world. The reverse could also be true that the religious individual is also a victim of circumstance at work. The non-religious person may be trapped in the secular world and see you as an outcast that doesn't have to be in the workplace. It is also important to recognize that even though the law may be against bringing religious beliefs or politics into the workplace, the reality is that it happens all the time. Just because it doesn't appear on the outside doesn't mean the problem is not occurring in the inside. The solution is to fix the problem from the inside and take out all the obstacles on the outside. Don't be satisfied with what the law may be asking from you. You may be considered to be the most tolerant of religion, belief, or other people's opinion, however, on the inside you know that is far from the truth. Getting to that truth takes acknowledgment but it is worthwhile to take the necessary steps outlined earlier and deal with it internally. It will be hindering in ways that you would not realize. It is also important to note that a good part of our communication is nonverbal. What we imagine can feed into our behaviors, actions, and can affect our feedbacks in ways that we may not be in control of. Why take the risk by not dealing with the problem?

CHAPTER 6

HAVE YOU BEEN ABLE TO UTILISE THE CLUES ON YOUR PATH?

One of our greatest gifts as human beings is the ability to store information and recall it when it is needed. However, many people don't recall the right information at the right time. They seem to forget just every useful piece of information related to their present situation. Many at work will easily recall all the failures that have been a problem. It is so crucial to train the mind to recall the details that will change our lives. Why do successful people pay zero attention to the impossibilities? Why do they focus on things happening while others are constantly looking at why things will not work? They are very quick to point out the negatives in every situation.

Sadly, with the aid of technology, we now have access to so much information that only encourages us to be isolated in our little corner, thinking that we are sufficient and possess all we need. Do we feel sufficient in all we do at work? Do we feel that nothing is lacking in our work/life balance? Is there something that we hope to improve in our careers or relationships? Is there anything that can be done to change the situation? Have we tried to fix the problem and haven't been able to solve it? To effectively change the mind is not as complicated as many people believe.

Let's Do A Reflection About Our Past

Let's try to recall what comes to mind from the past that we can identify as good? Can we list the things that we did today that made us happy? Are those things bringing us closer to our purpose? What about the favorite foods we've had? What about the relationship that made a difference in our lives? What sports have we enjoyed playing or movies we've enjoyed watching? Are we comfortable being alone? Recalling as many moments as possible is the first step but utilizing those moments is the key.

To utilize these memories effectively will require setting up the foundation that we have seen in Chapters 4 and 5. Every moment we spend in life should lead us to who we are and the purpose for which we are here on this earth.

Some may quickly point to the fact that they are not certain what their purpose is. They fulfill other people's dreams and not their own. A well-grounded purpose that comes from within will see that everything you do is never wasted. It may not be rewarded immediately but there is no way it can be a waste. Crossing a bridge that leads to the other side may not appear rosy but once you cross it, you realize life is so different from the way it was perceived in the past. What are the things that want to make you come to work? I used to tell my direct reports that if there is anything that will make them not come to work, please, let's talk about it. The caveat is that any frustrating human interaction is fixable but the science-related ones may be difficult. Scientific problems may appear easy once you figure it out, however, it is not a given. On the other hand, if it is easy, then we will be out of a job. How do we then cope when science, in general, is difficult? It could be expanded to say how can we cope when life, in general, is difficult? Can you list more things in your life that bring you joy?

The ability to recall those moments at difficult times is crucial. If during a difficult time, we are unable to remember who we are, then it is easy for any situation to become catastrophic. Imagine if the prospect of daylight is not known, how depressing would the night be? On the other hand, when the day lightens up, it doesn't appear like there will be night again. These are not things that we have not considered before. However, knowing how to implement these same principles in our daily lives will make a significant difference. Remember it took practice to acquire the skills that you have today. How could we just earn all our talent without any practice? The difference is to do the correct or surgical practice that removes all the obstacles in your career. Sometimes the obstacles don't have to be removed for us to be successful or be happy. What it may take is for us to recall the most beautiful song you've heard at the time of distress. Will that make our situation less important? Most people may think the opposite but the brain will not care a single bit about the situation but will respond based on what we attempt to recall. What about the times we've spent outside nature, can we recall how much peace we had? How come it disappeared so quickly when we're at work? Is there a possibility to recall something that will always remind us of the possibilities?

What Is A Successful Project That You Can Recall?

Unfortunately, projects come and go. Some may take a long time to be completed, others may not have a clear completion date. Some projects end not because they were not successful but because the market condition interrupted the completion of such projects. In all of these circumstances, we rely on the reward of satisfaction and count it as a victory or accomplishment. Is that a misnomer when success or failure is not guaranteed? How can we rely on the reward of such a project when we are not responsible for its success? Should we find a way to manage our expectations of project completion? Some have come to misguidedly rely on paychecks to make it a sense of accomplishment. Getting a paycheck is that something to look forward to? It may come bi-weekly, weekly or monthly for different people. What is the most precious moment you get to spend at work daily? Why should it not be the feeling of getting a paycheck daily? Will that minimize the worth of the paycheck? We can narrow our minds to look forward to only the paycheck but could get more reward by looking at the precious moments you get to spend and what you can do for it to be productive, fulfilling, or give us a sense of accomplishment daily?

Will We Want to Change The Perspective We Are Carrying Right Now?

To see the result calls for immediate practical steps. It is important not to look for external praise. Let it come genuinely from within. It is often advised that we fake it, till we make it. What that may be referring to is that we must practice in our heart until it becomes a part of us. For it to come naturally and not be chaotic, we must recall things that matter in the time of distress. Imagine those that have gone through very traumatic situations; most of them speak of situations or loved ones that they remembered carried them through their ordeal. Will that apply to your situation? The answer will be a resounding YES. The more we are able to stay on that thought process persistently the better our circumstances will become. If we give up halfway, it may be painful. The moment we don't fill our mind with that positive affirmation, what will come to fill it will be the negatives that could worsen the situation. That may not be the outcome that we will want to see. Sometimes the end may look unattainable but it doesn't have to be that way. The most effective efforts could be those baby steps that don't seem to be much but when continued, leads to the most dramatic results.

So far, we have looked at some aspects of recalling what we may have heard and how they may have influenced our decision-making processes. The general question that may arise will be, what about situations that don't fit into what we have talked about? It is impossible to cover all aspects of this topic. It is a good practice to invent the situation you want to take place. For example, I may have a supervisor who yells or uses curse words often. It is often said that fire should be used to quench fire. If you happen to yell at the same time he/she yells, then who will listen to the other? For some people, that could be the only way they know how to respond. However, that cannot be the only way to respond to such a situation. What about considering that this person may be trapped in their own world and can't get out of it. Continuously looking at it from that perspective may inject patience which is often missing because we want the result to be instantaneous. If we truly identify that we don't have the patience to wait for such results, we must try to practice patience using other scenarios. This rationale applies to the situation we are trying to overcome. Imagine when you are patient and doing the best you can, that individual, no matter how stubborn, would notice.

We often forget that no matter how powerful an individual is, they are still human and surely have vulnerabilities. It is important to be able to look for any vulnerability and utilize it. Some people use vulnerability to cause harm. You are much better off using it for the common good. As is often said, what goes around comes around. If things are not going the way you want them to, you could practice speaking softly when others or your supervisor is yelling. Will that change the situation or make it worse? Sometimes, things may get worse before they can get better but persistence will surely pay off.

Volunteering for a particular event or opening a safe space group to discuss the issues with the determination of getting a good outcome also helps. An important ingredient will be the determination to get a good outcome. I have seen how many of these safe space meetings that don't focus on the good outcome turn out to be more of a problem than a solution. The major obstacle is that a lot of things might be said that will not go down well with a lot of the listeners. Should we become reactional? The ability to control reactions in those meetings is a key element towards getting at a successful outcome. If whatever someone is sharing is looked at from an empathetic perspective, then the rest of the group must do that and provide some help and support. The support doesn't have to focus on the external responses but genuine responses from within. Our inner mind communicates more powerfully than we can ever imagine. We have all heard about the hunch that we feel when someone is genuine or not. Once we determine someone may just be using empty words, we are easily put off and nothing that person says becomes meaningful. It may be a wasted effort but why don't you spend the time to create that genuine or sincere motivation from the inside that will guarantee a good outcome?

Naming The Problems

Another aspect that is worth talking about is the fact that once we categorize all the things that we have identified, naming them will also help. For example, if one category involves blaming us for every fault that occurs at the work place, even though a lot of the blame is unfounded, not all of them are. Will we be able to genuinely identify those that are truly our fault and put them into a category of good blame? Those that are not our fault, we shouldn't read too much meaning into. They happened because someone was having a bad day. Give it a name – maybe, dumpster-blame because you can quickly trash it.

I will pay more attention to the genuine blame. Remember any moment we spend building ourself will not be wasted. Yes, it might have not come from the right person, or neither was it said respectfully. Could that be preparing for the next level or laying the foundation that we need for the success ahead of us? There is so much that remains unknown and we must be careful not to doubt for one second that what we are going through will not prepare us for a higher height in the near future. Think about the things you have recalled that went in another direction. This is important because finding a way to deal with the situation gives us semblance of understanding. The difficult aspect is not understanding what is going on, since our mind is not prepared to deal with the situation. You must have noticed that no matter how disjointed things may be, once we begin to figure out a process of dealing with it, it then becomes much better to handle and eventually we can find ways that it can be resolved.

So, what's the process like for your peculiar situation? The more you can define a process, the better you will be at dealing with it. If you throw something in a dumpster, we generally don't go back to look for it. Once we identify the dumpster items, let them stay in the dumpster, and not to second guess ourself about them. Some situations will certainly trigger us to go back and bring back memories from the dumpster because our brains don't throw things physically in the dumpster. Knowing that and deliberately directing those thoughts and tendencies is always valuable and lead to good outcomes.

What Physical Activities Can You Do To Practice Reorienting Your Thought Strategy?

You might go for a walk, go biking, hiking, swimming, laundering, and so forth. These are all activities that provide ample opportunity to train our mind in an impactful way. One essential element here is that there is virtually no side effect. If one approach doesn't work for you, simply persist or adjust to another activity where what you are trying to practice will be effective. For some people, meditation is the key to welcoming solitude and purpose. We are all very unique and what may work for one individual may not be the solution for another individual. The caveat is that we are all made with the same chemicals.

How do you modify what works for others to work for you?

CHAPTER 7

WHO INSPIRES YOU TO TAKE ACTION?

As an adult, if we look back at the number of books, newspapers, social media articles we read, and people we interact with daily, we'll find that there are so many attractions or distractions. It is interesting to note that there are people, who are deliberately manipulating those attractions behind the scenes. For some, it may not be people, it could be an animal whose behavior they have come to adore. Others might be the wonderful influence of nature and the powerful inspiration they derive from the wisdom and architectural beauty they admire daily.

In certain cases, we may not even recognize the influence. Can we make a list of the people or things that have brought hope to our life? What was it about those people that we admired? What do we dislike about those people? It could be our supervisor or an outstanding co-worker. What is it that we can pinpoint? I know some may want to look for perfection and look for the most powerful and influential person with zero faults. Just a gentle reminder that there is no perfect human anywhere. Our ability to judge also accounts for the criteria we are using to make those judgments.

I will suggest that the reader make a list of the most important things or attributes that make the most impact in your life. After you've identified those attributes, which of them do you want to have? Which of them do you lack but would love to have? Which of them is unattainable based on your ability? You can start reaping the rewards immediately by practicing with the low-hanging fruit of attributes that you bear already. Even if you're just unhappy with your present supervisor or co-worker, it doesn't mean they are not contributing anything to the system. Often, we are simply angry or discouraged by other peoples' actions so much so that we easily dismiss their contributions, talent, productivity, etc. This is one of our biggest mistakes. If you are unique, you must identify the very special things in your life that you can control and those you cannot control, which is by far a good majority of them. However, we often fail to acknowledge that we make the mistake of believing that we can be in perfect control of everything, only to discover that we do not. We meet different people of varying personalities that we can benefit from and it should not be taken for granted.

What are the odds that you come across people we don't get along with? What can you do to avoid them? This is something we often neglect and take for granted. How have we come to admire nature or any animal? What are the odds that we could have admired anything else? The opportunity for us to benefit from it will not last forever, and we can only harness it at very specific moments. It is essential to purposefully utilize the attributes rather than leave them to chance. The world is filled with so many influences and if we don't find a way to utilize what we have, the opposite becomes a reality. As a result, we are often incapable of doing what we want to do but are instead, constantly paralyzed by someone else's actions. We are in constant admiration of what we stand to gain from them. These people are humans like ourself and some of them will even tell us they are just lucky to be where they are. They may tell us they have no special talents. It is because we have chosen to rate and admire people based on very specific characteristics.

If we change the attributes, will we be admiring those people? The point is that a majority of the chemicals in their body are also in ours. As a consequence, our environment, what we choose to internalize, what we pay keen attention to will dictate how we respond to the situations in our lives. Think about a supervisor you have been at odds with because of their human interactions, only to find out that they are competent in other areas. It could be time management or an impressive dedication to duty. Can we look for the good or admire these individuals from that perspective? Do we have the capability to change this individual?

Can You Change Anyone?

I often see the desire in many people to do everything in their power to change others. I find it difficult to change myself all the time because some of my actions and reactions are beyond my control. Think about the destruction caused by drunk drivers. You are obeying the law and doing what you need to do and from nowhere, someone hits you with their car. What did you do to deserve that? Do we take all the responsibility for situations that we do not influence? In the same vein, we should make the most of what we have. It is often said that a drop of water makes a mighty ocean. But most people look for that instant breakthrough and change. The most effective change happens to those that start small. Starting small gives you plenty of opportunities to learn from your mistakes, which will for sure take place. Imagine starting very big and now you have all the spotlight. If you make a simple mistake, it becomes very magnified. You could have made the same mistake but no one would have noticed. So, we should be careful what we wish for. It's not a mistake that you are where you are today. You are complete but you might be using the wrong metrics to measure that completeness.

There are people we look at and see all their current contributions. The reason why those people might not have a direct influence on our current situation is that I believe we are more focused on admiring them and not deliberating on their strategies and values. There is something to be gained by looking at their strategies and values, and utilizing them practically. So, the attributes that we have come to admire were not cultivated by accident.

At some point in my education, I had to take some elective courses and I took American History even though I was in the Sciences. I read about Henry Ford's Assembly and how he compartmentalized the assembly line. This knowledge became very useful when I practiced chemistry in the laboratory. I wanted to be productive so badly. For me, it was a sense of duty to understand science and be good at it. I wasn't able to be the most productive in my laboratory but the determination and belief in my ability was key to my productivity. I started by noting all the steps I had to undergo, from receiving direction to planning the synthesis, organizing my procurement, and even confirming the availability of certain instruments.

What Are The Rewards Of Being Mindful Of Others?

I hated offending others deliberately, especially if I could avoid it. I planned my time around the availability of certain instruments. I would come a little early and run my analysis or stay a little late to avoid the traffic of people. Sometimes, I even took my lunch late. It became second nature with time. Starting was also the tricky part but once you nail it down, it becomes like a game. It becomes fun and stops looking like a chore.

I came to enjoy the planning and execution. You are directing traffic rather than the situation controlling you and not like situations that you seem to have zero control over. A crucial aspect was the planning. If you need to run several reactions daily, planning becomes the key to making sure you have all the material ordered ahead of time. Although it rarely goes well, adequate planning helps significantly. These were dynamic situations where the orders may be canceled. It was important to note when the order will possibly be canceled because there is new data.

So, the targets that come before any data were rapidly carried out because it may take some time for the data to show up. As the data comes, you look at the trend and see the direction things are going. Taking note of things around you could make all the difference in your situation in one way or the other.

Having listed all the factors that may have influenced your admiration and the people that bring hope to your life, were there politicians in your category? The issues of politicians are always mixed, in my opinion. The foundation of these politicians often dictates what their perceived contributions to the nation are. That is if they favor one side or both sides. Even when the benefits are there, they may not be widely recognized because of their political affiliations. In looking for people that bring hope to our life, one should also consider the negative biases that is influenced by the individuals' political orientation.

The true influencer in our lives should be determined by the contributions they make in our lives at present and whether they are aligning with our plans. Let it be geared towards the good though. If it is towards destructive tendencies, then we will find plenty of examples to follow or admire. Why do we do all we can to avoid such tendencies? Our innate nature sometimes is to recognize what protects us and our fighting spirit helps us survive whatever life offers us on a platter. However, this doesn't mean we cannot enjoy the brief moment we have on earth. When politicians speak, they often reflect what their interests are. Some people even say they follow a playbook. It is tempting to fill in the gap and move on but will that be a good foundation if we are in the workplace?

The problem with just filling the gap or space temporarily, is that it will not last and will need constant fixing. Therefore, why not spend ample time to lay a solid foundation that will last and produce incredible results? It is very possible to lay such a foundation, no matter how difficult the situation might present itself. Not spending the time to consider the things that attract us to those individuals will present a stumbling block in utilizing the strength that could be gained by taking a deeper dive into their productivity. Some people are more productive than others and without examining the reasons, they build false expectations. Take a famous person for example; someone who already has a structure in place to maintain their lifestyle and may just devote a few hours daily to studying a particular course so they can spend the rest of their time on many other projects. Their ability to perform well is heavily augmented by the unseen resources available. Does this mean that they should not be admired or acknowledged for their efforts? It all comes down to admiring what we hope to achieve in our lives. If we don't have such resources to begin with, how will we achieve what they are achieving?

Others come to truly admire religious leaders for their generosity and the good they have laid bare for all to see. So, how can that be applied in our workplace? The reality is that every good situation can be replicated in others if we find the right attitude or space to do it. You may not be required to talk about religion to people, however, the way we do the things we do will always be more powerful than the words we speak. It also depends on the listeners or recipients. It may not only be with what we do or say but may also have to do with the relationships we have created. If it is antagonistic, then nothing gets absorbed. On the other hand, a healthy relationship provides the needed motivation and influence for a lasting change. Once you identify the type of foundation you are in, it will be imperative to work on it to spark great and lasting change.

Recognizing the situation is the first step but doing something about it is also an important step. The doing is what scares most people but it shouldn't be if we are strategic about its execution. Not every action has to be chaotic. Is there a possibility of performing our most important actions and still be happy or not vengeful? Is the energy coming from getting back at someone or wanting to be the best? They may be good aspirations but have we truly examined whether we have the resources to do that or whether it's our life's calling? Will that help us discover who we truly are or who we would like to be in the future? If our purpose or goal doesn't reflect our true self, it becomes impossible to sustain true happiness. Others can see many accomplishments on the outside and may feel the admiration, or envy because of who we are but only us can truly understand those things are not exactly what they seem to be. The people that bring hope to our life could be our past or present colleagues that have become productive and have gotten our attention. Not everything about them needs to be perfect because the most effective people are often imperfect persons in the eyes of others. Making an effort to identify goodwill always brings in benefits, especially when it is needed the most. You might recall that attribute when we are anxious or worried and that could just turn our energy around. It may sway us from taking actions that may be detrimental. It is always the split-second decisions that do come to hurt us in the grand scheme of things. Why should we care? It will change our intents towards our daily life and affect the outcome of our life eventually. In the next two chapters, we will examine INTENTS and how to manage both the negative and positive ones.

CHAPTER 8

WHAT ARE THE THOUGHT PROCESSES HOLDING YOU BACK?

What are the negative intents that we think about regularly? Are we being constantly manipulated by those negative intents and are we unaware that they direct every move and decision we make daily? They may be controlling our relationships, the way we solve problems, and even our perception of others. It can quickly become a burden we are unable to free yourself from. What joy do negative intents bring us? Do we find ourself saying things that we end up regretting? Do we find that we're truly not proud of those intents when we truly examine them?

The solution to the negative intent does not need to be complicated. It is imperative that we are sincere, deliberate, and open-minded. After all, the key component of this book is about us identifying the things that we want to improve and be successful in. Even if we are successful now and think we do not need to improve on anything, that is a clear sign that we have a lot to improve on.

Imagine how many have made similar mistakes and each time we conclude that there is nothing to improve upon, we severely limit ourselves and refuse to take advantage of the many opportunities that come our way daily. How many discoveries do we see and ask ourself why no one thought about them? In improving ourself, there is no limit to how effective, happy, and successful we can become. This is why how we admire others and what we internalize about them is so important. If we set those limitations too soon, we will find ourself very content and it will just be a matter of time before we get used to our situation and become bored and uninterested.

What Can Infuse Energy Into Your Life And Make It Fun Even When Things May Not Be Perfect?

It is also worth noting at this point that those negative intents are not all that bad. Even when they are supposedly negative, they can turn around for the common good. Let's talk about the negatives. What may be negative for one person may not be negative for the other person. Imagine a co-worker who was brought up in a negative environment where gossips, fights, and abusive relationships are normalized; that person may quickly become accustomed to those behaviors. For such a person, abuse is just a way of letting steam out. It is just relieving the pressure that is inside and when they don't get to 'let off steam,' they become unhappy. How do we deal with such situations? There is not a one-size-fits-all. You may be the best judge but no matter what it is, there should be no doubt that such individuals should not influence our lives. What has that individual done to help themselves out of that situation? Have they encouraged good for themselves or the people around them? How open are they to honest feedback? Will they be willing to change their perspective? Some people are who they are. While we can be concerned about their behavior, we should also look at the reality of everyone's ability or limitation to change others. If we all can change one another, then we will all be the same. What would the world be like if that were the case? Certainly, there'll be no room for improvement, motivation, or innovation.

Although we want to change and improve, it is also important to understand the negative intent we have about ourselves or others. What negative intent can identify as a carryover from childhood? What negative intent came from the environment that we were born in? We can acknowledge that our environment has a built-in bias about certain things or people. Because we are so used to seeing it that way, it may have become normalized and we do not see the need to change. Many of these negative intents have also been solidifying in our minds for a long time. Removing them may demand deliberate effort. Again, removing them does not have to be painful, especially if we remove them using the right strategy, which is scientifically proven. Childhood intents are often based on fantasies that we make up or realities we created in our minds of what we want to be or want others to be when they don't do the things we want. What we may want could include things that are destructive in the long run but maybe fun in the short term. It could either bring instant satisfaction or gratification but will not be in our best interests in the long run. What are those negative intents that only bring short-term gains? Those are the ones I will prioritize because over reliant on short-term gains to escape stress can be very tempting.

The question that often accompanies this paradigm shift is, 'If I get rid of this intent, how do I retain the joy that I get from these negative intents?' If this is not handled correctly, it may leave the individual worse-off than when they started making the attempt to change. The reason is simple, once you lose something that makes you happy and you don't find something tangible to replace it with, you may come back at it with a determination to reinforce it because you may have concluded that there are no other solutions. The more we retain those negative intents, the more we will be controlled by them. The more we feed on them, the more they hold us back from becoming the best and happiest version of ourselves.

What about negative intent at the workplace? We looked at negative intent from a personal level but one may think that wasn't necessary and the workplace's negative intent should be our major focus. Remember our mind doesn't have or retain special chemicals for when we are at the workplace or when we're at home. The brain and body carry the same chemical around. We are who we are and anything we do in one area will influence the other in ways that we often ignore. The negative intent could be that we have a co-worker that may be causing so much pain for everyone else and we constantly wish that they were not around. Is that a reality or we can control who stays or who goes? Even if it is something that we can do, have we been able to put that thought aside and ask ourself what we can do to help that individual? For the most part, if the desire to change is not coming from a good space, it will not be effective. It is easy to give up when there is any sign of a problem. It will not work and it will be dealing with the problem from a superficial angle without truly addressing it at all. The negative intent could be that we have someone who is very productive and we find ourself playing catch up all the time. We wish they could slow down or wait for us to be at the top. There is nothing wrong with wanting to succeed and be at the top but it is not in our best interest to be negative. Why is that so? We have identified so many things that we are exposed to as individuals that are unique to our situations, our lives, our family, and so forth. The individual may be productive because they have enough time to plan or they may have a mentor guiding their every step. We are all exposed to different life challenges; how can I expect my situation to be exactly like someone else? How can I expect my productivity to be exactly like someone else's? Nothing wrong to desire to be at the top but it shouldn't be at the expense of getting at someone else to make them feel bad. We can work very hard and if in the end, we genuinely feel good about each other, then that's a win-win situation. At a minimum, that is what it should be about. What will we gain if, in the end, we are all wounded and battered and unable to enjoy the victories that we attain?

If we find ourself in such a trap of negative intents, we can turn them around. After prioritizing the ones that are the most devastating or most influential, we may want to take them one by one or take them together. All will depend on what we can manage.

We have mainly focused on negative intent in our thoughts, what about negative intent in our actions? What is the negative intent at doing something that you think is not in your best interest? The tendency to think and then act on it, only for you to realize it wasn't the best decision? Many of our actions may have fully grown in our thoughts and might lead to the actions that we take. We may intend for an action to represent what our desires may be but is any of that intent detrimental to someone else's progress? This is a common aspiration in science, where we look at what others have done and build on it. Often, we build on the loophole and uncovered areas and then, bring out our best ideas. So, part of negative intent is embedded in the way we think and improve. The key becomes whether we are truly improving for the common good or doing it to completely bring someone else down. It may be a thin line in some cases like in the story of a group of very competitive scientists. It is good practice to plan and set up reactions overnight. But the competitive spirit was so toxic that one of the scientists deliberately added water to the reactions of his/her co-workers' reactions. Excess water doesn't add value to most organic reactions. Instead, the reaction would fail when that happens and it was only later that the word came out that this individual was doing such a thing. It was a really negative situation, so why do we consider such an example? To acknowledge that we all have the same tendency to cross the fine line and lose sight of the bigger picture.

What is the value of negativity? Someone else's reaction failed, then what? What is the value in seeing others fail? Does that add any value to my life? What is the long-term benefit to me? The praise that comes with winning is very temporal. If we all realize that we are unique and special in our own ways, why should someone else not be special in their own way and have their own victory? Why should their value not be seen by the world? If we all have the same gifts, who would admire us? The world will be so boring if we all do the same thing, think the same way, and behave the same way. Will there be any motivation to improve? The benefit from someone else succeeding far outweighs the benefit of failure.

I know from a business perspective there is always the desire for the business to improve and beat the competition. There could be very limited customers if a business is not targeting the right people and pushing very hard to get a bigger share of the market. We constantly aspire to be the best at what we do and that is something that is required in business. Without that aspiration, the business will fail. Business has a collective goal and effort, and so shouldn't be entangled with personal day-to-day interactions. The mission of the company is to beat the competition and win. Personally, we must be the best we can be for ourself and the company. Notice, I deliberately included ourself first. Without us contributing positively to the company, we could easily be seen as a liability. Making sure that we are doing the best we can in a positive manner requires our thought or intent to build that foundation. It is a good thing to be alive and performing excellently well, since that will help us fulfill our overall mission in life, while at the same time fulfilling the goals of the company.

What Do We Do In Repeated Failures?

I was in a situation where every attempt at improving a method failed repeatedly. I set up a reaction with the good intention for it to be a success but the outcome led to negative thoughts and frustration. I thought to myself one day, 'Why am I so frustrated when things are going wrong? What do I really have control over?' At the beginning of the reaction, a lot of planning takes place. What am I missing in the planning stage? Are there steps that I am missing or not doing right? The first thing that came to mind was the fact that it shouldn't be something that tears down my personal life. If my thoughts are not stable, I would trigger more problems and shut down my thinking ability. It will affect my ability to move forward. I came up with two objectives for every reaction I set. The two criteria for success is to, at least, come up with a reason why the reaction will fail. At first, coming up with a scientific reason why the reaction failed was challenging but I never gave up. The more I practiced, the better I got at understanding the mechanism and with time, my failure rate went down dramatically.

Trying to figure out what went wrong forced me to dig deeper into the mechanisms. The more I thought about the mechanism, the better I could foresee problems, identify possible side products, and subsequently enjoyed the process. Often, the frustrating thing was not knowing what was going on and being unable to plan for the future. The second question I asked myself for each reaction was, 'did I set it up safely?' The overall reaction may fail but was it set up in a safe environment? This question is often overlooked. However, if the safety of my experiment is not guaranteed, there is a good chance that I may not be doing it for a long time. Safety just doesn't happen by accident; it is something that must be considered every time.

Many people feel frustrated for regularly attending a safety meeting. Safety meetings should be something we all look forward to because it is what helps keep the company going. Without individuals prioritizing safety in executing their tasks, there will be constant incidents that would hinder productivity and foster possible loss of business. Overall, safety is a collective effort from every individual. So, if I could answer those two questions then I will consider every reaction to be successful. From that perspective, most reactions become a success if I fulfilled those two criteria. This is so crucial because that perspective cleared my mind from the cluster of negativities. I was energized to do better the next day. I could easily come up with solutions to the reactions that didn't work. We have very limited time to think about the next step and finding a way to utilize that time positively, will add value to our life and present situation.

The other benefit is that I was able to focus my intentions and aspirations on the things I needed to improve upon. What I need to improve upon will definitely be different from what someone else needs to improve upon. If I had focused on beating someone else, I would have lost sight of what I needed to improve upon and be frustrated by their success. However, it wasn't about whether others were succeeding or not. I didn't care about anything else but improving my mind by constantly examining the literature to make sure my hypothesis was correct. I was often labelled the top performer in my group. There is no doubt that we can all be top performers but we must start by defining our success or failure from our perspective as unique individuals and not about someone else.

CHAPTER 9

DO YOU KNOW THAT EVERY NEED YOU HAVE CAN BE TRANSFORMED?

This topic may seem very simple and desirable by many. Who does not want to be happy or think about uplifting things? We all desire to think about success and productivity and be liked and admired by others. We want to be the best performers in all we do but how often are we disappointed by what our true actions are? How often do we find ourselves in negativity and feeling trapped in it? We don't need to think too hard to be negative and sometimes when someone is positive, we may feel irritated and guilty that the person might be exposing our flaws. We don't have to think negatively to be influenced by negative thinking. The number of negative news and stories is on a constant rise. Have you wondered why there is always something bad that we are so curious to listen to? How many planes landed safely today? I am sure it is not a number that you easily find because most people don't care about that and it is not something that people care to bring in the news. How many successful projects have we completed? We may not even pay much attention to them on a regular basis but how many failures have we had today? The ability to think positively is hindered by the many opposing forces that we are constantly bombarded by. Understandably, we don't have to pay much attention to the obvious expectations but instead, pay close attention to what needs improving. The unfortunate aspect of this is that one mistake or just one thing that may need improving could cast a complete shadow on all of our energy. It is something that the most successful people also suffer from. There is a gap in our minds where the feelings of incompleteness, inadequacy, and the inability to take constructive criticism may be a stumbling block for growth. How can we overcome that and replace it with positive thinking and unleash the hidden energy that we all possess? As we have done in other parts of this book, it is important to take stock of the positive intent you can identify in your life. What are those intents outside of our workplace? Are the outside intent more than the ones in the workplace?

Chances are that you may have other issues unrelated to the workplace. These outside influences may lead to a less harmonious or cordial working environment. If there is a lack, then there is a lot of work to be done but it can be completely overcome. We are not in this world to be utter failures or be barraged with negativity that we cannot overcome. If that is the case, why are we built in the most complicated or sophisticated way? Who will spend a lot of time building something only for it to be trashed? It makes no sense that we are in this world to only fulfill the negative aspects of our life. Let that sink in because it is something I have spent a lot of time considering even in the most difficult of circumstances. My overwhelming conclusion is that we are meant to be successful.

We are complete the way we are and just because things may not be going right at the moment doesn't mean it is over for us. Just because we don't see the prospect of success doesn't mean we will not be successful. The more time we spend thinking about what we can do to maintain that thought process, the more we will find that thinking with a positive intent all the time is doable. It is something we all desire even though it's not a natural tendency. It is not only when we feel like being negative that there is a problem but sometimes when we are complimented, we may just dismiss it and not internalize such compliment. When such a thing happens, how often do we step back and take the necessary steps to maintain such a positive compliment?

Positive Intent Is Not Something That Just Shows Up. We Have It All Around Us

Sometimes, we often have to look for it and bring it up in our subconscious. The more we fill our minds with the intent, the more examples we see to incorporate into our daily lives. The less we do, the worse our situation may become. The other day, I saw a video of someone demonstrating how positive intent works. The individual had a flask filled with mud, which signifies that we were born with the innate intent or desire to fight for survival. There is a significant tendency to protect the innate negativity that is exacerbated by our surroundings. A water hose was placed in this glass of mud and the tap was opened. It took a continuous flow of water for the glass to be eventually filled with clean water. Even with that, it was not completely clean. There was still some residue lying inside the flask. Imagine that we just cannot empty ourselves with all the negative intent and then fill our minds with positive intent. Sometimes converting the negative intent to a positive intent will be very effective since the negative intent is not going to just disappear. Imagine the mud was converted to a material that separates each particle and coalesces so that the clean water can push them easily from the bottom?

The negativity in our lives can be converted into positivity. It is important that we identify them just like we did earlier and begin the conscious rationalization. For example, one could have the negative intent of unhealthy competition with a co-worker. Only that particular individual knows how fiercely they wish that their co-worker fails so they can rise to a particular position.

At this phase, it may look benign because we are not doing anyone harm and no one can challenge us about it. Yet, this is detrimental to a harmonious and cohesive work environment and subsequently to the bottom line. The unhealthy aspect of it will certainly harm us in ways that we might not be able to imagine. That negativity creates so much limitation in ones thinking. If the person succeeds, it will hurt our feelings. But, what about positive competition where we are not hurt internally when an individual succeeds and we become more motivated to beat them when they succeed? Can this be done? The answer is a resounding YES.

Earlier on, we considered our abilities from a micro-level and discussed how unique the various parts of our lives are. We recognized that we are all imperfect. How do we improve our own imperfections if we are focusing on someone else's imperfections? The negative aspect will blindly obscure our ability to look at things from a holistic perspective. The individual who has succeeded has also conquered their limitations to increase productivity and their limitation(s) may be very different from ours. Why don't we focus on improving the different aspects of our lives instead of just focusing on the success of the overall outcome? The overall outcome happens after a while, but what happens on a daily basis?

Imagine if we can focus on the daily aspect, it will provide a clue as to what works in our individual lives. There is another point worthy of mention about the glass filled with mud example. Remember the exchange was slow because how much mud found in the glass will dictate how long the exchange will last. If the mud is filled, then it will take a longer time to wash off. Another aspect of it is that it didn't completely remove the mud. Residual particles were lying around in the glass. The process takes a while and, in our lives today, we expect an instant fix to every problem.

When it comes to making a change in our lives, is that a possibility? Some changes can be instantaneous and others take a little bit more time. When we categorize the intent that we can change in the short term, it will benefit us to focus on both the short and long-term changes. For example, a short-term change will be to not think negatively of the competition just because you want to win. If we do that, it can be replaced with thinking of that individual as doing the best they can, even though they may be going about it in a way that you don't approve of.

We can in the short term change our thought process. However, if we don't have a long-term strategy to deal with the triggers, it will be easy to fall into the same thought pattern we have just overcome. The long-term strategy could be to give it a name and remind ourselves about the trend in thinking. Finding a substitute to that pattern of thinking is a winning strategy that pays off in the long run. Have you considered the number of people that make resolutions and in a very short time lose the momentum? More people are failing to fulfill their goals than the ones that are succeeding. There might be some residual negative intent, however, if the positive intent is so dominating, it will negate any residual negativity.

The path to a lasting change is guaranteed when it is systematic and focused. If there is no strategy to overcome it, there will be no plan to overcome it when a challenge shows up. It will leave us unprepared for future challenges that we will certainly encounter. Naming is a very effective way of not only remembering our strategy but also reinforcing the plans we have to fix our problems. Another aspect of positive intent to consider when dealing with unhealthy competitions is to look at the situation more closely and identify if the individual you are having an unhealthy competition with is someone that you are friends with or someone you are not getting along with.

Often, we find that our relationships are a source for negative competition. If the relationship is cordial, we can discuss things and stay in the loop of what is going on. If the relationship is bad, then there is less communication and more second-guessing. Whatever he/she does is looked at from a negative perspective. Fixing the relationship will go a long way to bringing positivity to our competition. If that individual fails in what they are doing, how is that going to benefit you in the long run? How is that going to benefit the company in the long run? Is the character of the person so bad that the company simply overlooks it? If that was the case, then how do you measure their success?

The measure we set up for ourself determines how much envy we may generate and how much positive energy we have. The process can be effective when it is slow, sustained, consistent and thoughtful. If we give up on such a plan, then what is the alternative? To give up means that the dominant force that is built-in negativity will dominate and we know how much destruction that could cause. It will not only be at our workplace but will also follow through in every aspect of our lives, in everything that we do. It will show up in ways that we do not expect.

Is Your Job A Mission In Your Life?

The positive intent that is generated by how much we make doesn't last for a long time. The more money we make, the more we find ways to spend it. So, if our joy is tied around our paycheck, that could be the worst way to generate positive intent. It can be used in the short term. On the day we receive our paychecks, we can bring in all the positivity but we could recognize that we are not receiving that daily. What positivity is tied with our mission in life? We are not in that job because we are mediocre. We have a purpose irrespective of what we or others might think. We are not there by chance but for a purpose - to fulfill our life's biggest dream. What are the chances that another person will have that job?

There is no doubt someone else could be hired. They will not do it exactly how you would do it but there will always be someone else that could take our place. That is something to consider. We are there to fulfill our dream and that is just a transient point in our lives that doesn't last forever. People have come before us in the workplace and people will come after us. How do we then bring that into our intent and remind ourselves daily? What will be our legacy at our workplace? Will we want to be remembered negatively? Will the company want us back if you are gone? Would they want to hire us if all they can remember is negativity? Will positivity be something that we are all interested in surrounding ourselves with on a regular basis? This is tantamount to intrinsic job satisfaction.

There is another saying that misery loves company and if we catch ourselves in that trap, then we must snap ourselves out of it by taking the steps that we have talked about in this book. These are proven scientific steps that work. We don't even need to see the scientific evidence but look at the outcomes. They speak for themselves. How often do we want to be around someone who constantly tears us down? Someone who doesn't want to recognize any of our good actions? Will we want to hang out every day with someone who doesn't appreciate our efforts?

CHAPTER 10
WHAT ARE YOU NOT PROUD OF?

Negative responses are actions that we often come to either regret or not want to be part of. Some of the negative responses are things we deliberately do to get an edge over a particular situation. Imagine a situation where we are in charge of a document and feel protective over such a vital document. There is no specific guidance on how to take care of it and we are left to use our best judgment. At our discretion, we may choose to respond by hiding it from everyone else and people may need to scramble to find them. Is that a negative response to the situation? It depends on who you ask. Some may see it as protecting the organization, others may think we are just depriving them of access. How an action is received may determine whether a negative response is indeed negative.

The key is to be able to discern whether we are hurting the feelings of others or not. Not all our actions have immediate consequences though. Often, our actions have a later effect and that is why it is so crucial that we are in the right frame of mind. Many decisions are results of quick thinking. Imagine that we have to respond to an emergency and there is little time to think. We just have to respond to the thief entering our building. There is little time for us to think. We need to decide between calling the police to come for help or taking matters into our own hands? Given that there is a wide range of responses, depending on your particular situation, I will leave this for you the reader to consider. The circumstances we are faced with often dictates what our responses are.

Do we tend to get back at people, no matter the cost? This is an aspect that many of us are faced with at the workplace. First, why are there cases where we need to fight back, complain, let someone else know that we are not happy with the way things are going at work? There are many reasons why this situation will always exist. As a human being, you are very powerful, unique, and special, as we have seen in this book. The other reality is that we have limited knowledge and power and can only be in one place at a time. We can only speak one language at a time. There is no way to speak many languages to different people at the same time without involving technology. The point is that we don't often think about our limitations and simply expect perfection. That raised expectation often fails to meet our desires and we are disappointed by other people's actions. How do I prevent myself from responding negatively to situations?

Imagine you can't respond and don't have the ability to initiate a positive outcome. The moment we know we have the power over someone for what they may have done against us, the more tempted we will be to respond to what they have done to us. Remember that we could have very well been in the same situation as that individual. I know there could be an instant, where the individual is doing everything deliberately to provoke the situation. The fact is that both opposing parties are exposed to the same chemicals and psychological tendencies. Why do we act differently and respond negatively every time we are offended?

We all come to work with different backgrounds. We are faced with different situations outside of the work place. Some people may be dealing with a sick parent, an unstable marriage, or a relationship. Some may be dealing with situations they feel ashamed to talk about. Does that mean the situation will disappear because they are at work? Depending on what stage that person may be in life, they will always remember those negative feelings and people around them may act as a stimulus to their present situation. Even though we may have nothing to do with the situation, we are at the receiving end of such actions. The point is that we have the responsibility to refuse to be defined by what others are doing and avoid responding negatively. It may have nothing to do with us. Our life is so important and every minute is so vital that it is imperative for us to pursue our dreams than trying to respond to every negative situation in our lives.

Sometimes the tendency to respond negatively will test us, regardless of where we are in our life's journey. Irrespective of where we are, there is always room for us to improve. There will always be growth opportunities or temptations to overcome. When we are prepared to see these things in our lives, it helps set the expectations when they do arrive. If we have the mindset that it will always be a pleasant, perfect situation, that things will always align based on our plans, then we become frustrated at the slightest indication that things are going wrong. I had that weakness before and constantly imagined things to be perfect.

There were constant disappointments because things were not going well. For instance, I was always thinking that we should have all the school material and food we needed to eat since it is just the right thing for us to have. If

The Act Of Solving Interpersonal Problems

going to school is a good thing, why is everyone unable to do it? If work is a good thing, why does everyone who needs to work not have one? We may set ourselves up for failure without knowing it at all. Setting those high expectations will present many situations that will cause us to respond negatively. Thinking about the limitations that each of us have to live in. Is it possible to be faced with situations that will not cause us to respond negatively? Even though we might want the answer to be no, the truth is that it is good for us to have them. They will always be there in the first place.

Sometimes people respond negatively based on their prior experiences and they may think they are helping to make things better. We all have different perspectives and so we can definitely expect different responses from different people. It is important to recognize what things we respond to negatively and take action. It doesn't have to be a painful response. Once we rationalize what is going on, it becomes easier to respond to them. We must believe that about the negative impact our responses are causing. If they are something that energizes us, then we have to replace that response with something that will produce positive energy and overcome that other energy coming from our negative response. If we don't do that, it will be very difficult to take action on the things that we want to change. We are constantly looking for the things that energize us and make us feel good all the time. These are involuntary responses; except we are conscious about them and train our minds to respond accordingly.

There is no way any of us will be at the same workplace forever. No matter how good or bad the situation is. It will come to an end, one way or the other. What comes to mind in the split second we have to respond negatively? Does this fact come to mind or do we believe that the situation will last for a long time and we have to respond to make it right? Often, our sense of urgency in fixing things makes our situation much worse. While the sense of urgency is warranted, human behavior can be so complex that our best intentions can be interpreted negatively.

The more anxious we are for people's behavior to change, the more frustrated we may get when it doesn't happen. How long has it taken you to change a particular behavior? You may get some help that others may not have. You could be in a situation that you need to improve but you do not focus on that. I have realized that when people focus too much on what others are doing wrong, they may not be paying attention to what they have to correct in their own lives. If we all agree that we are imperfect and that there will always be room for improvement, it will make life better not only for ourselves but our families as well. If we can tackle the situation at work that is making us respond negatively, it will help our situation at home as well. It may provide a blueprint to what our tendencies are and how we can deal with similar situations when they arise.

Negative responses do not necessarily need to be directed at an individual only; they may be directed at what they perceived the company is doing. What tendencies do we always have to respond to what the company is doing with regards to pay, opportunity, bonuses, or the lack thereof? There are plenty of opportunities for us to respond negatively to the company's policies. Why am I so certain of this? Generally, company policies are not geared towards every individual need or desire. It may be that one person will have to make the decision even if the input comes from everybody. So, how will that situation not leave some people unhappy? The company can't please everybody. Therefore, some individuals are likely to respond to company policies negatively.

Do we want to find ourself in such a situation or will we do something about it if we find our colleagues in such situations? If we don't recognize it, chances are that we may be influenced by what surrounds us. The more conscious we are about the possibilities, the better prepared we are at responding. There will always be company policies we are not happy about. Policies that don't take our considerations into account. What we may need may not be what others may need or may not be in the best interest of the company. For example, I may want a pay raise that is commensurate to the hours that I put in. If you are on a salary, often, you find yourself putting in more hours than you can account for. Can you imagine the countless hours you spent brainstorming and implementing solutions? Will you be able to capture all those hours and ask to be compensated for those hours? Is that even feasible? I may think I deserve more money. However, when it comes to the grand scheme of things, more money may not solve the problem. Yes, it will always help to have more money but will not be the only thing that gets us from one end to the other in life.

Is There Certainty For You To Succeed In Life?

You are meant to succeed and be resourceful, no matter what life may look like right now. It is opening the possibilities and stretching our minds that will make the difference. We don't have to see it to believe it. What situation have we or others overcome by sheer hard work even if we didn't believe in the possibility at first? If any of the things that we now know were unknown, how would we plan for success? I don't believe we would have all the plans to succeed as we do now. How do we know all we need when most of what we see or do is unknown? We only experience an outcome but there are so many unknowns before the outcomes. Can we say for certain what happens to you or others in the next hour? We can project based on what we already know. There is so much going on in our body right now and how you respond to something may very well be determined by what your body is making right now. We don't often pay attention to all of these considerations. So, why do I need to understand every action to believe that I will succeed in life and pay attention to what is important? I do not need to understand everything that is going on to believe that I will have a good outcome in life. There is no way to understand everything. Given our limitations, we just have to work on understanding and internalizing that fact and take steps to practice living in this manner.

What are the steps that you can take to get rid of these negative responses, so you can reinforce the positive responses? We talked about how recognizing the existence of the worker is always the first step. Categorizing the negative and positive responses may lead us to the right direction. Write them down and remember you are the most important person in this situation, no matter who else is involved. If you are not aligning with how you feel and what is happening with you, chances are that you will not be able to help yourself or others in the situation. You're taking the time to lay the foundation for your growth, happiness and future goals. You are not here to fail but to get to a level that you can be proud of. It requires going through a process of self-awareness. The other aspect involves recognizing each person's uniqueness. Human beings are the most complex beings in the universe but nothing changes the fact that even the most educated or powerful may be doing things we are not happy about. We may not approve of their approaches or we may even wish that they did things differently. It is imperative to remember that the possibility always exist that anyone could succeed despite perceived differences.

How About Having A Non-Judgmental Attitude That Doesn't Leave You Upset With The Situation?

How about a situation where we can do what we need to do and be at peace with ourselves? Is changing someone's behavior the only solution that will suffice? It is possible to be at peace with ourself despite our troubled work situation? Once we've identified the situation, remember to think about situations that see the individual and not the upsetting things they do that you don't have control over.

Have you wished that your loved ones or children do things differently? Has it come to fruition? What reality are you faced with? And why are we not concentrating on the part that guarantees our mutual progress? Failure may not be an option for us in our lives. Our present challenges cannot completely impede our success if we are aligned to our destiny. We are more important than any failure that we can think about. No matter how informed we are, we cannot control the long-term destiny of others.

For our loved ones, can we stop them from getting sick or from getting into a bad situation? Can we stop them from not succeeding? The same applies to our lives as well. No matter how many people assume we will not succeed, it is wishful thinking except we hand them that power or authority. The words said to us as a child, how many of them have truly come to pass exactly as described? Why don't we spend the next chapter talking about the things that can ignite energy and purpose?

CHAPTER 11

FINDING THE OPPORTUNITY IN EVERY SITUATION

In the previous chapter, we talked about recognizing the negative responses both outside or in our current workplace. It is human nature to neglect one area at the expense of the other, however, the brain doesn't go to sleep because we are outside the workplace. We can attempt to put things away but that doesn't mean we cannot be reminded of the disturbing situation at work. Do we like going to work? Is there something that holds us back and make it almost unbearable to be at work? Is the difficulty coming from an individual or the nature of the job itself? Are we thinking about changing our job or moving to a different location? What alternatives can we think about?

Is staying the only option we have? Our wellbeing is a very important aspect, but at the same time, if we have determined that we cannot deal with it ourself, there should not be any hesitation to ask for help. The caution is that it has to be from someone who is trusted. I have witnessed countless times that most people do only so much because they do not understand and appreciate fully how complex, beautiful, and powerful they can be in the workplace. Other people may want to help or have the best of intentions but may be limited by an unhealthy work environment. Just knowing these facts does nothing except when they become part of our psyche. Even, if the situation has gotten to an unbearable level, there is always a workaround. It is essential that we determine whether we are no longer useful in a particular company, and do not allow the company to determine that. One might be let go at the wrong time.

Once we can provide positive responses and convert those negative responses from others, we will always be needed in one way or the other. In that way, we are in control of what we want to do or where we want to move to if the situation comes around that we don't like. We can quit at our own time but what can we do to provide that purposeful living? We've identified positive mantras that we can recite to ourselves so they become part of our thinking. Maybe there is room for you to join the gym or something that you haven't challenged yourself with. Is there a game or sport that you've come to love or a movie that you have come to be fascinated by? Remember, whatever it is, the work/life balance is important but at the same time, the company will not exist if we are not productive.

There are times when one may need to take the extra mile to get things done but it should never be at the full expense of our family life. Even at that, most companies expect the best output and this may eat into family time, which has become our modern reality. The ability to do it well may help free up some family time if we can be strategic about it. Once it is determined that we could multitask, we will be given more work to do. It will always be helpful to determine what that right balance is. Another aspect is to find reasons why we should be at work. If it is about the salary or temporal benefits, then, when those don't meet our expectations, there will be an automatic conflict with our goals and desires.

How Can You Identify Why You Exist In The First Place?

When you identify your true purpose in life, everything you do becomes truly part of what you were made to be in the universe. Who you are will not depreciate no matter what you may think about yourself or what others may think about you? For that to sink in, we can ask ourself these questions, how many people look just like us; think just like us and smile just like us? The more we internalize answers to these questions, the more we will focus on what we are doing daily. What are the things that are important in my life at the moment? What are the baby steps that I can take to move my career forward? It could be a learning opportunity, extra income, etc. Remember all our experiences are not wasted. What about our unique life story? We may think it is uninteresting but how many people can tell their own stories?

It doesn't matter whether we think our life may not be interesting. We don't have that final say. Our life story could be what someone else needs to hear. How many famous people never imagined it was ever possible for them to be famous? The reverse can be true as well. The point is, why don't we stay on the positive side that helps with our wellbeing? Why go through life with all the negative feelings of sadness, negativity, or just wishful thinking that things will never get better? That a situation doesn't go our way doesn't mean anyone should suffer the consequences. If the world operates that way, then only specific ideas will rule the world. There will be no motivation to change or improve on anything.

Are We Too Dismissive?

Sometimes, we refuse to internalize certain things and instead, we treat them superficially. In such instances, we never get to reap their full benefits and only get superficial results. In my abject poverty, these thoughts became internalized and the more I saw the world that way, the more I turned off the outside noise and distraction and focused on the important stuff. The situation became a building block to my next level, even though I had no idea what the next level was. As I look back, it was the only way I avoided being killed by my destructive behaviors. Just knowing the fact or how to respond to a situation is not enough. We have to see it as part of our reality in life. Remember that our brains do not have special chemicals for every situation. As a consequence, how you regulate those chemicals is important, and once you figure out a way to do it, you are training your mind to handle it when the next crisis arises.

It took me years to define what success means to me. I had to figure out what I have control over. The things that I don't control but are manageable, I made an effort to do just that. For those that are out of reach, I simply ignored them because there was no point in expending my energy in the wrong place. At such a time, when if our gut feeling gives us a go-ahead, then we must pursue it, even when everything around tells us it is impossible. If we look around, there are plenty of examples of people that others have doubted their success but this didn't stop them from dreaming. It doesn't matter if no one agrees with that dream. We are limited by our ability to determine our destiny in the first place. I know we are told the opposite, which is completely false. The fact is that if we align with who we are and what we are meant to be, we can assure ourself that we have complete control over our destiny. However, if we are going in the wrong direction, then just saying that is not something that will get us to the greatness we envisioned for ourself. Getting that alignment to the person we are meant to be is crucial and very doable but it requires that you be purposeful about it. If we decide to talk about something that didn't seem doable; how long did it take you to go to school and get the education that has allowed you to read this book? Why don't we see that all it takes is being purposeful?

You Don't Need To Be The Best To Succeed.

You may or may not need to be the best in a given situation because it doesn't matter. What matters is that you are reading this book right now and it took some effort to get to this chapter. In fact, it took a lot of effort in your continuous learning from childhood to be here. What about finding that space to understand why you truly exist on the planet? Because, once you align with that, you will have the energy you never thought possible. Unfortunately, we define our success based on what others think success should be. It is generally based on what is popular opinion and what others may have achieved, even with the foundation or breaks they've had. Aligning to who you are is all the foundation you may need. It may not be the loudest voice in our lives, except we train ourselves to listen to that innate voice that no one else but us can hear. Why pay attention to what others are listening to and not to our unique voice? Your job is just a bridge to who you are and who you will become. The number of challenges right now cannot have the final say or determine who you will become. If that were true, then let's try to multiply the successful people.

Why are we still figuring out how to motivate people in their workplace or life? Why are we not learning to treat each other better and are instead getting more destructive? One half closes their ears to the opinions of the other half. Are we forgetting that because we disagree with someone's opinion doesn't mean they are incorrect? If we all agree that we don't know everything, then how are we so certain that what we are saying is the absolute truth? Why don't we entertain the fact that the opposite opinion could very well be true in time? Why does it have to be a zero-sum game? Are we already defining our failure to see where others are coming from? Can we leave room for possibilities so that we can focus on our innate direction that may not always be clear?

If we are to be happy and succeed with our goals, we must accept that not every situation deserves a response. We may need to ignore certain things because we just don't have the time or capacity to address every problem that comes our way. The number of interactions that we engage in is a lot and the reality is that not every one of them will go the way we want them to go.

Can we learn to internalize these principles and think about holding in our urge to respond all the time. I used to be a problem solver and it was exhausting doing it every time. Ten chances to one, I was not able to solve every problem. If I have acknowledged our differences, then there will be different ways problems will be solved. It is the same thing in the real world. The focus has to be balanced between what comes from within and what comes from the outside. What comes from within focuses on what needs to be done and what direction we should be going if we pay attention to it closely. Having said that, if we haven't taken the first steps to understanding who we are and who others are, then the right foundation may be non-existent. The ability to get the right energy may not be there and without the right foundation, it may not lead to the right direction.

The question is how do we know we have the right foundation?

The sincerity and focus we place on determining good or bad is very important. How important? Think about things that have turned out to be contrary to our expectations - the relationships that are not thriving right now; the future that doesn't seem to be on the right path; the career that may not be going in the way we expected it to go etc. You are not on this planet by mistake, despite what others may think. We have a unique purpose to serve and contribute to our workplace or family. That is not something that should be thrown around lightly. Learning takes a lot of man-hours and still, look at the things that we learn that we may never use. If knowing who we are is that important, why not spend time figuring that out? It is possible to know exactly who we are and why you we here on this planet. It doesn't mean there will not be times that we will doubt that. However, the more it is reinforced in our minds, the clearer we will see things align every day. The opposite can also true. The more misaligned we are with our identity, the more we see things that go in the wrong direction.

The search for our identity and purpose can be unsettling. If we have constantly depended on outside forces to shape and direct our life, then it might look very strange. If that is not working for you at all, will you want to continue in that direction? Do you want to live other people's lives? How can you be happy and fulfilled when we are fulfilling someone else's aspiration? The first time I started recognizing my identity was challenging, because the concept was new to me. We are trained to listen and follow instructions and so we get so used to it that we stop to look for things to learn and internalized. Most of them are what others may have learned and we spend a lot of money and time to get what others have been able to overcome. Why does it need to be that expensive if we are special in our own right? Have we been convinced that we are the problem and must seek a solution? Look at the rate of our development and yet, our interactions still leave much to be desired.

There is so much hatred, backbiting, insecurity, insincerity, frustration and so many other vices pervading our land. Despite all our training, these vices still exist and, in some cases, are even getting worse. Imagine if we all know our unique identities and also appreciate each other's and their contributions, will our situations be different? Is that even a possibility? If we can reduce or minimize the vices, it will be a significant win. No matter the hatred people may have for one another, we cannot let it win at the end of the day. There is so much wasted energy on things that we have no control over.

When I flew to Nigeria in my teenage years, I believed that I was on my way to a better education and better living conditions and I was so excited. The most interesting aspect of that plane ride were the moments when the plane would pass the clouds or thunderstorms as I indicated earlier. At that time, I enjoyed going through the bumps and shakes. When we passed those turbulences, I would wish that we came across more. That was a moment I kept in my mind for a long time and didn't utilize it until one day in my adult life. I was traveling from California to Madison and we stopped at O'Hare airport in Chicago. People that have traveled that path understand the frequent weather issues that arise during the journey. I wasn't comfortable with the shaking and thunderstorms then. It was no longer fun and, in some cases, I ended up regretting the flight. During this particular flight, I recalled my childhood experience. I didn't consider what might go wrong as the plane went through the storms when I was a child.

But as an adult, I have been sensitized to hearing about plane crashes, infrequent or not. I had a monologue during which I reminded myself there was nothing I could do at the moment that would help the pilot. Also, no other person can control the plane except the pilots. Because they knew what to do, they were the ultimate controllers of the plane. So, no matter my original fears, I decided to focus on what I can do to enjoy that flight. The journey immediately changed my perspective again and in subsequent flight I started enjoying plane rides. I must admit though that I don't enjoy it as much as I did when I was a child. This story is synonymous with many of our life's events. How many things can we truly control? How many people can we truly change? Do we have the magic wand for all situations?

We are constantly warned of danger here and there. We are being told of many problems and what to do to fix them. Are we truly focusing on what we can control? Are we living a fantasy thinking that we can control everything when something as big as an airplane can only be controlled by a few people? It is so important that we know this and manage our expectations. All my worry and panic may do nothing to control my life's journey. I recalled traveling in a bus filled with vacationers. The driver was a little reckless and will overtake other vehicles in the narrow roadway. One instant, our vehicle tilted a little bit and there was shouting of joy. It was like it should continue to repeat itself. Now, no matter how worried I was at that time, I had no control of what the driver was doing. I could yell and be angry about the situation, it may release some steam of anger but may not change the situation in an instance. When do we determine that remaining calm is the best approach?

Some people will yell all the time no matter the circumstance. However, does that provide any advantage to their situation? Some may argue that they may get an instance reaction. Looking at it closely, do we take into account the health implication of constantly increasing blood flow and releasing those stress hormones all the time? Its consequences may not be immediate and this is something that is constantly ignored and the majority will go for the instant gratification. This example may reflect many occurring situations that we face daily at work or at home. We are sure we can control most situations and we try our best to do so. Sometimes the best control is no control at all. It can be very effective and powerful. We can take out the burden on ourself when we realize that we are not entirely in control of every situation, no matter how badly we think we can control them. If everyone has that power, then the world will be in a constant problem. Even the workplace will be in constant turmoil because we are all passionate about what we think is right.

It is not what society has conditioned me to believe or live by. Not what I have been told is success. Not what I've been told to crave for. The moment we take the steps identified in this book could be the moment things will begin to turn around in your career and life in general. You are not here to be mediocre. You are not here for other people. You are here to be yourself and contribute to life. It will be the catapult that takes you from one level to the next. It will be that inner peace that is unstoppable. It may be temporarily affected due to what goes on around us but it will not be permanently derailed. You will have a path to always come back to. It will be that pendulum that swings you back to who you truly are and what you have contributed to this planet.

A journey like this will need reinforcement. You must revisit your progress along the way. We know that our brains and minds appreciate repetition. Without repetition, many concepts will be impossible to understand. Without repetition, it will be difficult to get good grades in class. Only a few people do not require repetition in everything they do. I know I wasn't born a genius and had to learn things along the way. If you know you are not (even if you do believe you are), I believe it is important that you revise the things in your life that you have identified to have paramount importance because they give you ultimate peace, productivity, and success not only in your career but your entire life.

CHAPTER 12

TRANSFORMATIONAL LEADERSHIP DOESN'T HAVE TO BE A NIGHTMARE

In this chapter, we will examine what needs to be done. Many people feel frustrated about taking action because it may require them to spend so much time and resources to achieve a particular goal. I hope you've been able to see that it doesn't have to be so. These are principles that are reachable by anyone since they are concerned with who you are as an individual and what you are going through at that moment. In as much as it is very doable, it is time consuming taking classes in schools or colleges or even at our workplaces. Imagine that no one pays attention to what was taught in each training session, where would we be in our careers? No matter how difficult your situation, you are unique the way you are. There will be no need to repeat the same strategy and expect a different result. A minimal adjustment to your work/life balance may be all you need to do, to see the difference that you once thought was impossible. There is value in what you are doing right now in your career. Our work is a mission that takes us from one point to the other. It was never meant to be the end. Just saying it will not make the difference but organically incorporating it in the good and the bad times will make all the difference. Just knowing it during the good times will leave us highly unprepared when the difficulties show up. Given that we humans are fallible, these concepts may disappear the moment they are needed the most to make a significant difference.

The moment of joy or motivation that we have identified by observing or reading about others can whisper the exact phrase that changes our response to different situations. If they were negative, then the negative response may be dominant. However, if they were positive, the positive response will likely dominate. Irrespective of the outcome of our responses, it is also imperative to remember that we are not perfect humans. However, when we don't meet our expectations, it should be acknowledged and then, we move on. The ability to continue practicing is very important. Giving up may just accelerate our decline in the worst possible way. The ability to start again becomes very difficult. Why should we give ourselves so much empathy and why should we always try again?

We saw the complexity in our identities and the things we do not control. How then can we expect to control all possible outcomes? I know sometimes the answer is "but"; this is an answer I believe to be the most damaging word to our success. The moment we begin to give exceptions as to why we shouldn't be empathetic to ourselves, it becomes almost impossible to achieve our true goals in life because we will be on the constant move and can't figure out what may be going wrong. The question is, 'Can we figure out everything that will go wrong?' When we should draw the line is a personal decision but I believe that if you've taken to heart what you've read in this book, you will have clarity about setting that boundary. Your boundaries will be different from that of others. However, the need to take action is not something that anyone has an exception to. If you want to see the kind of result that takes you from one difficulty to another, where you are sure of their outcomes, then you may need to go over the concepts in this book; taking note of areas that are most challenging, and working on them using the principles you've learned. It is practically impossible to not get a positive result.

Why am I so emphatic? What you've learned in this book is that you are the only one that thinks like you, speaks like you, and was born at the same time you were born. Spend some time to think about that and practice the steps outlined in this book. It has worked perfectly for countless others and you will not be an exception. You will find value in trying, rather than spending so much time and money doing it in ways that haven't been successful. Take action that gets you where you want to be irrespective of who you use to get there.

My goal in writing this book is not just to offer a solution for every individual. It is to allow people get to where they can be by consulting with who provides the most help.

The point is you are too valuable to be treated any less in the workplace.

CHAPTER 13

YOU'VE JUST UNLOCKED THE SECRETS OF GREAT LEADERSHIP

I have seen too many situations that cause needless pain and suffering in the workplace and in people's lives. I have also seen how situations like these are transformed with a different perspective that no one envisioned they could reach. No matter how impossible our situations may seem, no matter how long it has taken for them to be resolved, there is always a path to their resolution if we dare to try a new approach. Why do you use the same approach over and over, even when it has never delivered a solution? Time is a concept that can be viewed from different perspectives. At your most stressful moments, do you recall what time really is? Beyond our planet, time is meaningless.

When we spend a day or a month, or even a year dealing with a problem in the workplace, but compared that to time beyond our planet, we could easily see how meaningless time is beyond our own perception. Yes, the problem may be painful but it will not last forever. It is a bleep in time and will disappear almost like it never existed. Now we have seen how to turn our situations around in this book.

We didn't choose who we wanted to be when we were born. It is imperative to understand who you are from within. Most people will ignore it to their peril. Given how complicated each of us is, why should we not spend time to understand who we are? If something is complicated, we should at least try to pay attention to it and then find some meaning to it. It is no different with our personality. You were also exposed to situations during birth or at your workplace that tried to define you. Won't we want to pay attention to our external influences? The more we put these pieces together, the better clarity we gain at home and work. What we see outside our sphere begins to validate who we are. Getting a solid foundation helps to minimize the negative intent that always comes our way. The negative intents are not limited to our innermost feelings but we can be receivers of them. It doesn't have to be what defines us because many positive intents will override the negative intents.

If we treat it like our lives depend on it, it will no doubt begin to shape every situation in our lives.

It is imperative to solidify these principles because whether we respond negatively or positively depends on the foundation we have laid. Without a solid foundation, it becomes very easy to go around a cycle trying the same things and having zero results. A solid foundation will allow you to pause certain situations that would have triggered a negative response. Often, that brief pause could make all the difference.

Just knowing how to respond doesn't guarantee that we can respond positively during difficulties. We have seen how quickly our knowledge tends to disappear when we are stressed. To avoid that, we must learn to address our troubles. Again, this requires serious action, one we can incorporate into our daily lives.

You are special and should consider applying the principles you have learned in this book to your daily routine. I hope you take the necessary steps to address the situation. Once you do, I have full confidence in a long-lasting resolution.

ACKNOWLEDGMENT

I acknowledge those who have been most influential in my life. Dr. Malynn Utzinger and Dr. Timothy Weitzel for their mastery of emotionally and socially intelligent principles that lay the foundation to self-discovery.

Hearty thanks to Dr. & Mrs. Joel R. Walker, the Usona Institute and Promega Biosciences family.

A special thanks to Prof. Dr. Gregory R. Cook, who welcomed me into his research laboratory with a special treat that unleashed my scientific possibilities.

To Mr. and Mrs. John F. Turay for countless hours of editing and encouragement in the writing of this book.

To the publisher of this book, I am eternally grateful.

ABOUT THE AUTHOR

Robert B. Kargbo, Ph.D. has been in a Supervisory role for over two decades. He is a trained Synthetic Organic Chemist, who has been involved in drug discovery for over a decade. He was a lecturer at the College of Medicine and Allied Health Sciences (COMAHs), University of Sierra Leone. He has over one hundred articles that have been published in reputable journals. He is an Editorial Board Member for several high-profile journals. Furthermore, he is a member of the Emotional and Social Intelligent Group. Currently, he is the Project Technical Lead in Chemistry, Manufacturing and Controls for the Usona Institute. In addition, he is a Senior Investigator, Chemistry New Product Development for the Promega Biosciences Inc.

THANK YOU FOR READING

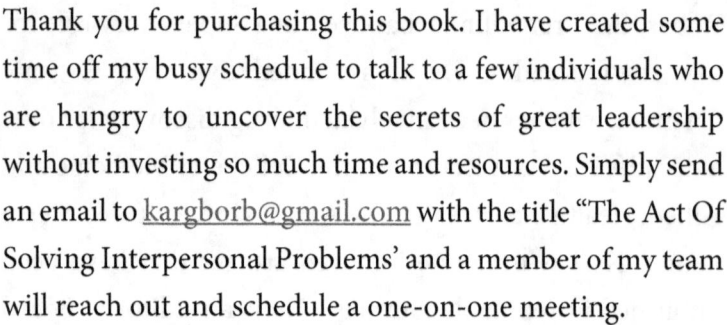

Thank you for purchasing this book. I have created some time off my busy schedule to talk to a few individuals who are hungry to uncover the secrets of great leadership without investing so much time and resources. Simply send an email to kargborb@gmail.com with the title "The Act Of Solving Interpersonal Problems' and a member of my team will reach out and schedule a one-on-one meeting.

To learn more about what we do and access free resources, visit

LEADERSHIP QUALITIES NO ONE HAS THOUGHT ABOUT THAT BRING HIGH PRODUCTIVITY AND TRANQUILLITY.

◆────────•────────◆

Do you know that many leaders are not fully satisfied with their accomplishments? Their subordinates are neither satisfied nor happy but are constantly under stressful working conditions, constantly annoyed, unfulfilled, depressed and are desperately looking for a change? I used to think that leadership was a very difficult and stressful journey until I uncovered the practices that allow me and many other scientists to become highly productive content leaders within a short time. As a scientist, I have had to deal with many fellows whose social lives have been transformed by these principles. Scientists are generally viewed as socially 'wired,' bookish, uptight, 'too serious,' gritty, nerds, etc. If their lives can be transformed, I don't think there is anyone who cannot benefit from these principles.

- Have you thought about the reward of knowing why you are who you are?
- Do you ever think about why others behave the way they do and how enlightening it will be to know where they are coming from without confrontation?
- How do you read between the lines at the workplace without causing problems and still be impactful?
- How do you compete fiercely and still leave you and others genuinely happy?
- Have you thought about how you will feel if the most difficult problem at the workplace is solved amicably?

This book provides the blueprint that every successful leader has adapted but hasn't been articulated in a way that people understand until now. The investment you make today by grabbing a copy of this book will do much more than you envisaged. **It makes no sense that you are not born to succeed**.

www.ingramcontent.com/pod-product-compliance
Lightning Source LLC
Chambersburg PA
CBHW070648220526
45466CB00001B/339